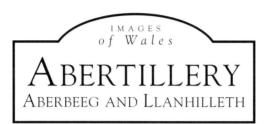

IMAGES
of Wales

ABERTILLERY
ABERBEEG AND LLANHILLETH

Blaina & District Farmers' Association

ELEVENTH ANNUAL

SHEEP DOG TRIALS

Wednesday, Sept. 20th, 1933,
at TY-ARTHUR FARM, Abertillery

(Near Roseheyworth Colliery, and on the side of the main road, Blaina - Abertillery.
'Buses pass the Farm. Kindly lent by J. H. Wallace, Esq.)

PRESIDENT - - - SIR JOHN BEYNON. Bart, C.B.E.

Class 1. OPEN SHEEP DOG TRIAL.

1st Prize £5   2nd Prize £3 10s.   3rd Prize £2 10s.   '4th Prize £1 10s.
5th Prize £1   6th Prize 15/-   7th Prize 10/-   *Entrance Fee 5/-*

Class 2. NOVICE SHEEP DOG TRIAL.

PRIZES: 1st £3 10s.   2nd £2 10s.   3rd £1 10s.   4th £1.   5th 10s.
Entrance Fee 3s.6d.

Class 3. LOCAL NOVICE SHEEP DOG TRIAL.

(Confined to a radius of three miles of Blaina Church).

PRIZES: 1st £1.   2nd 10s.   3rd 5s.   *Entrance Fee 1/-*

Class 4. SPECIAL CLASS for PIT HORSES

not exceeding 14·2 hands, at present working in the collieries under the Ebbw Vale Combine.
Prizes kindly given by the Officials, and exhibits judged by the Company's own judge.

Class 5. SPECIAL CLASS for PIT HORSES

not exceeding 15 hands, at present working in the collieries under the Ebbw Vale Combine.
Prizes kindly given by the Officials, and exhibits judged by the Company's own judge.

To commence at 9 a.m.

Admission to Field - - - Sixpence.

ENTRIES to be sent to the Secretary: **E. J. Andrews,**
Mount Pleasant Farm, Llanhilleth.

REFRESHMENTS ON GROUNDS.

"THE SOUTH WALES GAZETTE," Ltd., KING STREET, ABERTILLERY.

Poster advertising the sheep-dog trials held at Ty-Arthur Farm, off Rose Heyworth Road, Abertillery, 1933.

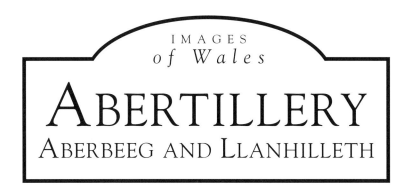

IMAGES
of Wales

ABERTILLERY
ABERBEEG AND LLANHILLETH

Compiled by
Abertillery and District Museum Society and Simon Eckley

TEMPUS

Coombes' Dairy, seen here at the opening of its new bottling plant, the only one in the Abertillery area, Pantypwdin Road, 1949. It was run at that time by Mr Hubert Coombes whose father had founded the business. Previously, the dairy had operated from far smaller premises at the back of Duke Street. Fred "the Milk" Howells stands right of picture watching his brother, Bernard filling another crate. Fred spent all his working life in the milk trade with the exception of wartime service as a driver in both North Africa and France.

First published 1995, reprinted 2003

Tempus Publishing Limited
The Mill, Brimscombe Port,
Stroud, Gloucestershire, GL5 2QG

British Library Cataloguing in Publication Data.
A catalogue record for this book is available from the British Library.

ISBN 0 7524 0134 3

Typesetting and origination by Tempus Publishing Limited
Printed in Great Britain by Midway Colour Print, Wiltshire

Contents

Foreword 7

Introduction 9

1. A Coal-powered Economy 11

2. Rail and Road 37

3. A Community and its People 51

4. Trade and Industry 79

5. The Strength of Religion 95

6. Education 107

7. Service to the Community 115

8. "A Really Good Time Together" 129

9. Song and Performance 139

10. Sporting Life 149

Acknowledgements 160

The familiar face of Ken ("Ski") Turner of Rhiw Parc Road, Abertillery, pictured after finishing his shift at Six Bells Colliery, 1970s. Due to ill health "Ski" finished work at No.5, Six Bells in 1981. His family still lives in the Abertillery area: his son, Mark, who followed his father down the pit to work in No.4, now lives in Blaina as does his daughter, Diane. Of the other four girls, Margaret, Sue and Kathryn all live in Abertillery while Pat has "migrated" to Aberdare.

Bert Snellgrove of Arrail Street, a well-known face in Six Bells for nine decades, seen here in the 1950s.

Foreword

By Herbert S. Snellgrove

It is an honour to be asked to contribute a foreword to this new book by Simon Eckley and the Abertillery and District Museum Society. As these photographs clearly show, the Museum has, over many years, been successful in preserving much of the rich history of the area.

My memories of Six Bells and Abertillery stretch back over many years often to some of its darkest moments; to the stoning of blacklegs in the 1926 Strike, to the humiliation of unemployment and the means test in the 1930s, to the 1960 colliery disaster, when, as Treasurer of the Lodge, I had the sad task of distributing, to widows and fatherless families, some of the monies raised by a shocked public.

Yet, if I am pressed to sum up these valleys' history and to pick one characteristic which has reappeared in one generation after another, it is that of a fierce community spirit and determination, laced with that black Valleys humour, to overcome whatever Nature or governments could throw at us. I well remember, as a young man in the '30s, us boys getting together to travel the length and breadth of Monmouthshire giving concerts, doing turns and raising funds for our people back home. These towns and villages have never sat back and waited for the worst to happen but have gone out and created a community and culture the equal of any in this country. We have built institutions, churches, clubs and societies of which we can be well proud. It was government by the people for the people and we tried never to forget the importance of that fact.

As Chairman of the Council in 1958-59 I had the privilege of representing the area. One day I was to attend a local school to be presented with a book of poems by the children. They had been told that a very important man was coming to meet them and word got to me from some of the fathers, miners with me at Six Bells, that there was plenty of nervous excitement about at the prospect. The day went well and the children were all on their best behaviour. What makes the event stick in my mind and makes me chuckle is that I was told later by a friend that his son had come home most disappointed from school. He had said: "Dad, he can't have been all that important, you only put his windows in last week." That is, perhaps, where power should lie, in the next street.

Finally, let me once again congratulate the Museum for producing this marvellous book. I hope you, as readers, will spend many long hours of enjoyment turning its pages, in reminiscing, in thinking of how things were and how they still can be.

H. S. Snellgrove.

The Foundry bridge, Abertillery, 1920s, with the bakery of E. Jeffries & Son, to the left. Their slogan at the time was "You have tried the rest, now try the Best".

Introduction

Through its selection of photographs and illustrations, the great majority of which have never been seen in print before, this book has tried to capture the essence of Abertillery, Aberbeeg and Llanhilleth over the last century.

Many pictures have been chosen from the collection of Abertillery and District Museum Society, which has long been building up an excellent photographic archive in addition to the treasure trove of local artefacts on display in the museum building in Abertillery. First formed on 30 September 1964, the society is now over thirty years old. Since its inception it has been run entirely by enthusiastic volunteers and continues to provide a vital base for the discovery of the area's history, by young and old alike. I am indebted to all the members of the society who have contributed to the book, and, in particular, to the Curator, Mr Don Bearcroft, for his constant assistance and advice. Without him the book would doubtless have spent many more months in preparation.

Local collectors have also supplied many cracking images of the area's past and I am extremely grateful for their willing help with the compilation of the book. My thanks go especially to Mrs Pam Hopkins, for many years a professional photographer with the studio of Raymond Hawkins in Abertillery, for giving permission for the inclusion of material from her own extensive collection.

To do full justice to the richness of the area's history a volume several times thicker than this would certainly be needed. That is a publication which I hope someone will embark upon in the not too distant future. Abertillery is a fascinating and, potentially, highly rewarding area for detailed historical study.

Despite occasional periods of depression and industrial unrest, Abertillery was, through the late nineteenth century and early twentieth century, a boom town growing rapidly along with the demand for coal from its pits. In 1920 the number of miners in the South Wales coalfield reached its peak at 271,000 men. At the end of that year, before the vicious 1921 cuts in wages, Welsh miners were able to earn as much as £5 a week with mining companies receiving profits of 10 shillings for every ton of coal they sold. South Wales was producing 20 per cent of Britain's coal and its ports handled over 60 per cent of the country's coal exports. Abertillery, with its concentration of population, was well placed to take advantage of this economic prosperity becoming the "shopping centre of the western valleys of Monmouthshire".

However, as John Davies has written, the history of industrialised South Wales is "a striking example of the peril of having too many eggs in one basket". The situation began first to deteriorate substantially through 1924 and by August of the following year 28.5 per cent of miners in Wales were out of work. With South Wales so dependent on international craving for her high quality steam coal the permanent slump in this demand, due largely to the increasing use of other sources of energy epecially oil, produced severe economic and social problems in the Valleys. Between 1923 and 1934 the number employed in Wales fell by 26.2 per cent and in 1932 Monmouthshire was suffering from an unemployment rate of over 40 per cent. Collieries introduced short time working and some, as was the case at Six Bells, were forced to lie idle for several years until demand improved slightly as the 1930s progressed. Without flourishing collieries subsidiary industries and the retail trades were hit very hard.

With the glory years of rapid economic expansion clearly over the tide of people turned and years of migration into the Valleys became long decades of drift away in search of opportunities elsewhere, often in the increasingly prosperous south-east of England. From an all-time height of 38,805 recorded in the 1921 census, the population of the Abertillery soon began to fall, down to 31,790 in 1931 and thence steadily downwards toward the present, relatively stable level of about 18,000.

However, there is long history of fighting this decline stretching down to the Miners' Strike of 1984-85 and the present-day. In February and March 1935 South Wales rose en masse to protest its neglect by the government. The failure to understand the area's problems and the harshness of efforts to curb expenditure through the Unemployment Assistance Act and the means test had provoked extreme bitterness. Mass action, reminiscent of the Chartist protests a century earlier, took place as thousands marched on the Abertillery offices of the Unemployment Assistance Board and the police courts. "We'll make Queen Mary do the washing for the boys when the revolution comes", they sang.

These men and women refused to give up the fight for human dignity, for a chance of life without the crushing burden of poverty where work and opportunities were there for all those who wanted to take them. As Bert Snellgrove suggests in his splendid foreword to this book the people of these valleys traditionally hated the prospect of going "cap in hand" and their resilience and inventiveness in the face of poverty must be celebrated. They had built their own distinctive community and wished to determine its future. Perhaps they realised that if it could not pay for itself, then this control would pass elsewhere.

To make managable the photographic record we have divided the book into ten chapters. But, of course, these themes of coal, sport, public service, etc. can rarely be looked at in isolation since they were repeatedly interwoven and interlinked to forge the community we have known. Some of these many connections are indicated through the book and many more are there to be discovered. We have tried to build on past publications and provide further fresh insights into the history of people and places in the area. I very much hope that each reader will thoroughly enjoy this journey into the past and emerge fully aware of what the district has achieved and what it is capable of in the future.

One
A Coal-powered Economy

Sinkers at the Six Bells pit of John Lancaster & Co., c.1890.

Llanhilleth Colliery,
JUNE 15th, 1901.

APOLOGY.

I, the undersigned ALBERT COLES, of Preston Street, Abertillery, hereby express my regret that on June 13th, 1901, I committed a breach of Special Rule Number 91, established under the Coal Mines Regulation Act, 1887, by having in my possession in the Mine belonging to Messrs. Partridge, Jones & Co., Ltd., a Pipe.

And I hereby tender my sincere Apology to the Owners, the Officials, and my Fellow Workmen for so doing.

I further agree to pay the sum of Ten Shillings towards the Library Fund as proof of my penitence, and to pay the cost of printing this Apology.

I also undertake, in the future, to faithfully observe and support to the best of my ability, the Rules and Regulations of the Coal Mines Regulation Act, and the Special Rules established thereunder.

I also agree that a copy of this Apology shall be posted up at the Mine as a Warning to others.

Witness my Signature this 20th day of JUNE, 1901,

ALBERT COLES.

Witness to the above Signature—**DAVID DAVIES.**

Sinking work at Six Bells pauses briefly for the photographic record, early 1890s. The perilous nature of such work is well illustrated by the over-crowded "bucket" suspended from the temporary wooden headgear. These were brave men. Often sinkers worked in specialist peripatetic teams brought in to develop the south Wales coalfield from the older, declining mining areas of Somerset and the Forest of Dean. They often formed the first wave of in-migration which saw many thousands from the West Country of England flock to the new mining communities of south Wales in search of work.

With smoking a potentially lethal activity underground Albert Coles was perhaps fortunate to escape dismissal from Llanhilleth Colliery in 1901.

Budd's Colliery, Aberbeeg, c.1905.

The site of the above Aberbeeg North colliery site some years after the headgear had been dismantled, 1930s.

Gray Colliery, Abertillery, c.1910, now the site of Abertillery Comprehensive School. Powell's Tillery Colliery Company began sinking here in 1885; the pit was in production until 1938, thereafter being maintained for a time as a second exit for the Vivian Colliery. The Gray, Penybont and Vivian collieries were all linked underground. Clearly visible on the hillside behind the colliery are the blackstone quarries above Gellicrug first opened in the early nineteenth century. Their stone was used in the construction of one of the docks at Newport.

Powell's Tillery Collieries' ambulance team, winners of the J.S. Martin Shield for the Southern Mines Inspection District, pictured at Newport in 1911. From left to right, back row: John Gibbs (Brigade Secretary), T. Evans (Manager), W.J. Little, J.T. Gill (General Secretary), John Matthews (Superintendent), William Lewis, W.H. John (Colliery Agent and later M.P. for Rhondda West from 1920–50), William Williams. Front row: Dr Rocyn Jones J.P. (Chief Surgeon), F.N. White (H.M. Inspector of Mines), William Stewart J.P. (Managing Director), Dr F.J. Browne (Inspector of Team), Allan Powell (Captain).

Cwmtillery Colliery, c.1914. Mining activity in Cwmtillery dates back to at least the early 1840s when the Blaina ironmaster Thomas Brown was active in the area in an effort to secure a cheap and reliable source of coal for his Works. In 1850 the first deep mine in the area was sunk here at Cwmtillery on the land of Tir Nicholas Farm. It was a major thrust of the industrial revolution into what was to become the Abertillery district. However, as in many other colliery ventures in these early unregulated, pioneering days, coal was not extracted without considerable human tragedy. In 1857 and 1874 explosions at Cwmtillery killed 13 and 20 men respectively and in 1874 an underground accident claimed the lives of 6 more men.

Cwmtillery Colliery, c.1920. In 1852 the colliery was taken over by John Russell, a Risca coal-owner and under him production was dramatically increased. In 1864 the South Wales Colliery Company was formed to take over the Tir Nicholas workings and its first managing director was Colonel Lawrence Heyworth, also of Risca.

Penybont Colliery, originally known as the Tillery Colliery, c.1914. This pit was developed from 1860 by Powell's Tillery Colliery Company. In 1893 the granary and stable buildings (both only recently demolished) were used to house the troops dispatched to the area to quell the hauliers strike of that year. The site is now occupied by Tyleri Court day centre.

Inauguration of the new colliery sinkings undertaken by John Lancaster & Co. Ltd at Aberbeeg, 4 December 1920. The site, however, was never developed into a working colliery.

Colliers at the Lancaster pit, Six Bells, 1920. Note the caps worn underground before the introduction of protective headgear. The colliery reached peak manpower figures in 1914 when it employed 2,857 men and annual coal ouput once stood at a staggering 600,000 tons per annum. However, the slump in demand for coal led to short-time working from 1928 and eventual shutdown of the colliery between 1931 and 1935, forcing many colliers on to the dole or out of the area in search of work (see p.98). In 1936 control of the pit passed from John Lancaster & Co. to Messrs Partridge, Jones and Paton, owners of other collieries in the Monmouthshire valleys and it remained in their hands until nationalisation in 1947.

Lancaster Colliery, Six Bells, c.1920, with the washery, right. On the opposite side of the river to the colliery another headframe is clearly visible. The Ordnance Survey of 1880 indicates a disued coal pit in this area and it seems probable that what we see are the remains of the water balance shaft for this earlier enterprise, exploiting the Tillery seam.

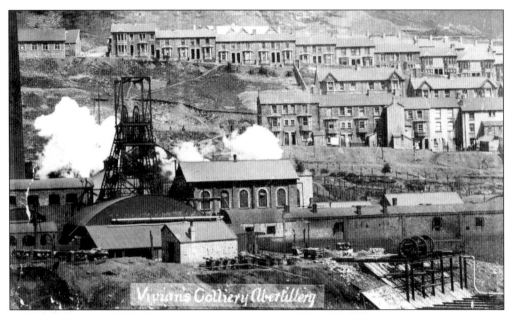

Vivian Colliery, c.1920. Coal was raised here from 1890 until 1958 when the pit became a downcast shaft for the Six Bells Colliery. Note also the two buildings top left, then used as a wheelbarrow factory, and the gables of Bryngwyn School just visible above the roofs of the top row of houses.

Vivian Colliery, c.1920. Part of the area once covered by the colliery is now occupied by Abertillery leisure centre.

Rose Heyworth Colliery, Abertillery, c.1925. Sinking of Rose Heyworth was begun in 1872 by the South Wales Colliery Company with the first coal being raised in 1874. Its name was taken from the wife of chairman and managing director of the company, Colonel Heyworth.

Rose Heyworth, 1980s.

South Griffin pits, outskirts of Blaina, c.1925.

Holidaying pit ponies during the annual shut down of the pits in the last week of July and first week of August, fields above Cwmtillery, 1930s. Though some ponies sadly went blind after years of working in the darkness of the mines their excitement, when released each year for two weeks of freedom and sunshine, was always immense.

Old Arael Griffin Medical Aid and Hospital Fund

President, R. BOWEN, Vice-President, S. WILLIAMS

Secretary - JAMES HILLIER,
124, Richmond Road, Six Bells,

Rules to govern Payments to Members
January 1932.

(1) The above Society provides that where a member requires an Artificial Leg, such member shall receive assistance up to the value of £5.

For Artificial Arms...up to the value of £3

For Artificial Eyes...up to the value of 10/6

For Trusses...Single Truss 5/-, Double Truss 7/6

For specially-made Surgical Boots...Single 25/-, pair 45/-

For Elastic Knee Bandages...5/-

For Ankle Bandage...3/6

For Straight Jackets...£3

For Abdominal Belts...15/-

For Arch Supports...8/6

Spectacles up to the value of 7/6 will be provided where a member is suffering from Nystagmus, or as the result of an accident, provided he has been ordered same by a fully-qualified person.

In each case the member must give to the Secretary a Doctor's certificate and prescription, whose duty it shall be to obtain the member's requirements direct from the makers. Where the cost exceeds the amount allowed under the above headings, the member must hand the balance to the Secretary to enable him to place the order.

No member shall be entitled to receive more than one benefit under the above headings.

The opening page of the revised 1932 rulebook for the Medical Aid and Hospital Fund of the Arael Griffin Colliery, Six Bells.

A well used and picturesque Llanhilleth Park, c.1930, with the colliery in the background. The splendid Miners' Institute, opened in 1904 and sadly one of the few remaining "stutes" in active use in south Wales, is still the major centre of the local community and heavily involved in much charity work. It houses a library, a doctor's surgery, the headquarters of Llanhilleth Athletic F.C. and remains a meeting place and social centre for ex-miners. Under the chairmanship of Mr W.E. Smith, himself a miner at the Llanhilleth (No.2) Colliery until its closure in 1969, a cenotaph was recently built in the grounds of the institute to commemorate the sacrifice of the village in the two world wars.

Opening of the new miners' institute in Division Street, Abertillery, 27 August 1955.

Enduring the wait for news following the explosion at the Six Bells Colliery, which claimed the lives of 45 men on 28 June 1960.

Six Bells, 28 June 1960.

Six Bells, 28 June 1960.

First body to be interred, Brynithel Cemetry, 1960.

Name	Age	Occupation	Reference No. on Plan No. 2
Ivor James Baiton	48	Cutterman	45
Daniel James Bancroft	46	Collier on Panzer ...	36
Robert Charles Brown	35	Roof Control Officer ...	20
Frank Cooper	44	Supplies Man	29
Joseph Corbett	50	Haulier	43
Thomas George Crandon	46	Repairer	33
Walter Thomas Davies	34	Borer	28
Royden James Edwards	27	Repairer	8
Percy Gordon Elsey	52	Repairer	30
Albert John Evans	34	Packer	23
Leonard Keith Frampton	29	Collier	17
Albert Gardner...	59	Assistant Cutterman ...	44
George Goldspink	37	Repairer	14
Clive Alan Griffiths	18	Prop Checker	13
Vernon Alexander Griffiths	33	Deputy Grade I	11
Ernest Victor Harding...	51	Deputy Grade I	41
Idris Jones	57	Packer	15
John Percival Jones	56	Repairer	38
Joseph John King	56	Packer	37
Dennis Edmund Lane	19	Wireman	1
George Henry Luffman	55	General Worker	7
Telford Cecil Mapp	42	General Worker	32
Herbert Amos Mayberry	55	Dumper	5
William John Morden...	52	Engine Driver	4
Sidney Moore	54	Repairer	3
Colin Malcolm Donald Morgan ...	26	Repairer	16
Colin Reginald Morgan	22	Assistant Repairer ...	26
Ray Martin Morgan	44	Repairer	27
Islwyn Morris	44	Deputy Grade II... ...	31
Anthony Verdun Partridge	20	Assistant Borer	12
William Henry Partridge	45	Borer	19
Trevor Paul	25	Assistant Repairer ...	10
Wilfred Alfred Charles Phipps ...	60	Cutterman	6
Albert George Pinkett...	45	Collier	18
Frederick Rees	37	Fitter Grade II	25
Mansel Reynolds	21	Measurer	21
William Glyn Reynolds	21	Assistant Repairer ...	24
Wilfred Hughes Thomas	57	Repairer	40
Arthur Waters	37	General Worker	34
Phillip John Watkins	53	Engine Driver	2
Wilfred Weston	47	Water Infuser on Panzer...	42
Frederick White	58	Under-manager	35
William Burdon Whittingham ...	55	Assistant Repairer ...	39
Richard John Williams	51	General Worker	9
John Woosnam...	24	Fitter Grade I	22

The men killed, 28 June 1960.

The funeral procession passing the colliery, Six Bells, 1960.

Return of the Six Bells Colliery party which visited Czechoslovakia, Newport station, late summer, 1960. A selection of fifteen men and officals, carefully representing the lodge, older and younger miners and relatives of men killed, were invited by the Czech government and the miners of that country for a period of recuperation after the tragedy of the Six Bells explosion. From left to right, back row: Brian Matthias, Mick Williams, ? Lewis, Tommy Williams, Aneurin Bancroft (who represented the sons killed), -?-, Stan Hewitt (deputy overman representing management), Reg Mappe, Dick Hoskins, ? Legge. Front row: Eddie Jones, Reg Lane (representing fathers of men killed), -?-, Bernard Rees (Chairman of the N.U.M. lodge at Six Bells and leader of the group), Bert Snellgrove (lodge treasurer). Once in Czechoslovakia the party was treated royally by the authorities. Part of the visit was spent in a convalesence home in the mountains with an international gathering of miners from not only Czechoslovakia but Italy, Belgium and Russia as well. Initially, the language barrier proved troublesome but the Welshmen, with Bert Snellgrove at the piano, started up the "hokey-cokey" and broke the ice in fine style. Visits were also made to the opera, a new but thoroughly enjoyable experience for the boys, and to the Pilsen brewery, where Bert, a life long abstainer, remembers the willing help of Dick Hoskins in downing surreptitiously (so as not to offend anyone) his quota of beer. While driving around the country the coach carrying the Six Bells group was involved in an accident in which a little girl broke her leg.

Fortunately, Tommy Williams, ambulanceman at Six Bells, was on hand to set the fracture and such was the quality of his work that a personal letter was sent from a grateful Czech hospital congratulating him.

Opencast coal production on Llanhilleth Mountain, c.1950, with the now demolished Cross Fence House on the right. Mrs Smith, then owner of the building, refused to move from her home despite all the inducements and threats the mining company could muster; the work of extraction, therefore, had to be diverted around her.

Don Bearcroft taking a break from Saturday afternoon maintenance work at Six Bells Colliery, c.1963. After nationalisation substantial modernisation was carried out at Six Bells. Electrification of the shaft winding was introduced, although by the late 1970s, as part of the National Coal Board's streamlining measures, all coal mined at Six Bells was being wound at Marine Colliery, Cwm, in the Ebbw Fawr valley. In 1979 manpower stood at 638 producing 111,000 tonnes a year (cf.p.17) with estimated reserves of 5.4 million tonnes (50 years).

The new Gleithabel coal plough at Cwmtillery/Rose Heyworth shortly after its introduction as part of on-going modernisation of the colliery, c.1970. On 21 November 1960 the neighbouring mines of Cwmtillery and Rose Heyworth were officially combined as Abertillery New Mine. A £3 million scheme had involved the driving of a new 1,096 metre (3,595 ft.) drift mine in order to integrate the two collieries and streamline coal handling. By 1979 the underground workings had spread beneath an area of eight square miles with pit manpower standing at 987; a further 88 men were employed in the washery.

Coal conveyor, No.4 pit, Six Bells, c.1974.

Shale tips disfiguring the landscape at Cwmtillery above the lower of the lakes, c.1960. The Cwmtillery Reclamation Scheme began in 1974 and continued up to and after the closure of the colliery in 1982. The former presence of the colliery is now indicated by the two pit wheels erected in 1987.

Rose Heyworth site, early 1980s before the construction of the new road and the demolition of the colliery buildings transformed the appearance of the area.

Pantygasseg private level, 1981. From left to right: John Desmond (owner/manager), Jim Whitcombe, Billy Smith (leading Danny the pony who still works at the mine. His mother, by the way, was the determined woman of Cross Fence Cottage on p. 29), Eddie Woolfall, Stephen Desmond, -?-, Michael Desmond, Dennis Smart. Together with his cousin, Mike, Stephen Desmond has now taken over the running of the level from his father.

Stephen Perry admires the fossilised *Sigillaria* tree trunk found in the Meadow Vein horizon, Six Bells Colliery, 1982. The fossil was removed entact from the face and transported to the mining museum at Nantgarw where on arrival it was sadly found to have broken into pieces. However, surveyors from Six Bells performed a remarkable job of reconstruction and were able to return the fossil to its original state using resin from shot firing. From Nantgarw the trunk was taken to London where it starred on the BBC's *Blue Peter* show. The programme's producer was quick to comment on the amazing way in which the fossil had been removed from the mine and transported to London without falling apart. If only he knew!

Gwent and Rhymney Food Fund, Miners' Strike 1984–5. From left to right, back row: Ron Stoate (Penallta), Keith Edwards (Britannia), Gerald Law (Nantgarw), Ernie Sanger (Nantgarw), Ray Gurmen (Markham), Gerald Edwards (Bargoed), Roy Williams (Six Bells), Des Aylesbury (Six Bells), Alan Sandel (Celynen North), Ray Lawrence (Celynen South), Ian Cole (Blaenserchan). Front row: Sam Holland (Markham), William Greenaway (Bargoed), Dai Edwards (Marine), Bernard Skinner (Treasurer), Ken Jones (Chairman), Jim Watkins (Food Co-ordinator), Gethin Jones (Rhymney Valley), William Parry (Tredegar Combine), Howard Miles (Tredegar Combine), Tony Davies (Blaenserchan).

Postcard designed by Peter Cormack and published by Stoke Newington Co-operative Party for the Gwent Food Fund, Miners' Strike, 1984–5.

The resplendent banner of the Blaenau Gwent lodges of the National Union of Mineworkers (now on permanent loan to the collection of Abertillery and District Museum) held high during the 1984–5 Miners' Strike. The marchers are pictured near Blaina as they follow the path taken by the 1839 Chartists from Brynmawr to Newport.

Abertillery Women's Support Group in Cwmtillery, Miners' Strike, 1984–5.

Scaffolding rises around the headgear of Six Bells in preparation for demolition, 1988. What the community had been desperately fighting to prevent had become unstoppable.

The flattening of Six Bells colliery, the last working deep mine in the Abertillery area. Picture by Pam Hopkins.

Rithan level, Llanhilleth Mountain, c.1982 with pony, Sam and Clive Dee and Paul Lions of Trinant. The level was opened in 1980 by David Warren of Argoed Farm, Brynithel following in the traditions of his grandfather, Ivor and father, Vernon, both of whom had worked in the local collieries. Private, often family, levels such as this have always been part of the rich culture of coal in the area, pre-dating and now out-living the deep-mining operations on the valley floors. Sadly, these levels, too, are now under threat in the new energy marketplace which sees little use for coal.

Two
Rail and Road

This postcard, actually published in Scotland, c.1905, illustrates Abertillery's reputation as a major social and nightlife centre for the western valleys of Monmouthshire, where the last train was packed by revelers returning to their home towns and villages.

The symbiotic relationship of coal and the steam locomotive is evident from this 1910 view of the south side of Llanhilleth Collieries. In the early 1850s Powell Bros sunk the first deep mine at Llanhilleth to a depth of 240ft and a second shaft was added in 1865 to improve ventilation. In 1890 the lease was acquired by Partridge, Jones Co. Ltd and they sunk a new steam coal pit (Llanhilleth No.2) on the eastern side of the valley (right of picture). By 1850 a railway link had been opened between Blaina and Newport allowing coal to be transported down the valleys to the docks and export markets. It is no co-incidence that the rapid development in the area of deep mining for steam coal also dates from this time (see p.15). In 1794 a branch of the Monmouthshire Canal had opened to Crumlin and a network of tramways was soon built linking the head of the canal with Aberbeeg and Ebbw Vale. However, while the canal, and an expanding tramway transport system, were able to cope with the coal traffic generated by the many small levels already in production in the area they would have been swamped by the vast tonnages extracted by the deep mines. Throughout Britain in the second-half of the nineteenth century the same pattern was repeated with the rapid eclipse of the canals in favour of the new star: the steam locomotive. Note the mineral track to the right of picture; this connected at Swffryd with the main line to Pontypool. Although not normally used for passenger traffic because of the steep gradient, it was pressed into service during the Second World War as a access line for employees of the Glascoed Munitions Factory in Pontypool (better known as the "Dump").

View of the railway running north from Llanhilleth towards Aberbeeg c.1910. Llanhilleth Workmen's Hall dominates the left of the picture.

Fred Day (in white coat) with the delivery "steamer" of Phillips Brewery, Newport, en route to the Walpole Hotel, Llanhilleth, c.1920. Fred was a brother of Tom Day from James & Day (Bakers), Aberbeeg.

Depot staff at Aberbeeg station, 1920s.

New engine sheds, Aberbeeg, c.1920. By the 1910s the sidings here had become very cramped with eighteen locomotives operating from the old, one track, Aberbeeg shed which dated from the middle of the nineteenth century. The Great Western railway (G.W.R.) operators of the Ebbw Valley line, estimated the cost of new accommodation at £23,650 and authority for construction was granted in 1913. The First World War intervened, however, and building was delayed. When hostilities ended in 1918, the Aberbeeg project still remained high on the priority list for the G.W.R. and on 29 June 1919 the new sheds were officially opened.

The railway sidings at Aberbeeg junction, 1930s. Here the line divided into two branches following the Ebbw Fawr and Ebbw Fach valleys.

Browns Corner, Six Bells, pictured by Abertillery photographer, Tom Tarrant, for use in a road safety campaign, 1930s. Tarrant had a studio in King Street next to the old offices of the *South Wales Gazette*. Notice the coach, one of many run by the family firm of Ralph's, a well known and well-used bus company in the Abertillery area.

The quickest way to Abertillery from Newport or any point in the Eastern or Western Valleys is by

RALPH'S SERVICES

ABERGAVENNY
BRYNMAWR
WAENAVON
NANTYGLO
BLAENAVON
BLAINA
BOURNEVILLE
CWMAVON
ABERTILLERY
ABERSYCHAN
ABERBEEG
PONTNEWYNYDD
PONTYPOOL
PONTYPOOL ROAD
LLANHILLETH
GRIFFITHSTOWN
HAFOD-YR-YNYS
NEW INN
CRUMLIN
SEBASTOPOL
NEWBRIDGE
PONT-NEWYDD
CROES-Y-CEILIOG
ABERCARN
CWMBRAN
CWM-CARN
LLANTARNAM
CROSS KEYS
MALPAS
RISCA
NEWPORT (MILL ST.)

RALPH'S
BUS SERVICE
ROUTES

Buses every Half Hour from Newport after 7.28 a.m.

Time Tables and Full Particulars post free.

RALPH'S GARAGES LTD., 155 Somerset St., ABERTILLERY.
Telephone 58.

Map illustrating the extent of the services provided by Ralph's Garages Ltd in the 1930s. This successful motor vehicle business was started in 1912.

Cyril Collier of Collier's Garage, Abertillery, pictured left, on a motoring holiday near Sidmouth in south Devon, 1930s. The business was first started in 1907 by Cyril's father who gradually expanded from building push-bikes into car sales. In 1925 Collier's became the Ford agents for the area. By the 1920s one of the first petrol pumps had been installed outside the garage in Hill Street, Abertillery. Previously, petrol had to be bought in cans of one or two gallons. For many years Collier's also had a car showroom on Somerset Street (towards the Cenotaph) as well as a bicycle shop (run by the family in what is now the pet shop).

Mrs Williams, mother of Percy and Albert (right), c.1935, about to embark on her first plane ride – her eightieth birthday treat! The flight was operated by Western Airways Ltd and ran from Cardiff to Weston-super-Mare. The Williams brothers of Princess Street, Abertillery were well-known local characters who from c.1930 ran a "pop shop" next to the Old "T's" (Old Tylerians Club) on Somerset Street. This was also known as "Tricky's" after the nickname one of the brothers had earned performing stunts in the swimming baths. About 1960 they both retired, subsequently spending time touring this country, and also America, by car.

Locomotive at Cwmtillery Colliery, c.1930.

"Winchester Castle" locomotive, Great Western Railway, c.1961.

44

Locomotive driver, Bob Fowler of Aberbeeg at Old Oak Common sheds, London, c.1961. He is seen here preparing a Castle class locomotive for a trip on the main line. Bob started as a cleaner and "call-boy" on the Great Western Railway in 1943 working his way up to fireman and eventually to senior driver. He finished work in 1991 at Newport after $48\frac{1}{2}$ years service to the railways including almost twenty as local representative of ASLEF, the rail union. Always a keen rugby player, Bob was for many years Chairman of Aberbeeg R.F.C. He is also a steward and active member of the congregation at Aberbeeg Methodist Chapel.

Work on the new foundry bridge well on the way, c.1950. This was the first bridge of pre-stressed concrete to be built in the country. It was intended to ease the bottleneck that had built up with the increasing volume of traffic seeking to use the old foundry bridge opened in 1898. Note the dead end at the top of Division Street.

A huge crowd turned out to witness the official opening of the new Foundry Bridge, 18 July 1951. The ribbon was cut by Cllr Florence Brown, the first female Chair of Abertillery Urban District Council (1951–52) who can be seen, centre of picture, in her chain of office.

Some of the first traffic to flow over the new bridge, 1951.

The beauty of steam is captured as a coal train crosses the magnificent Crumlin Viaduct (speed limit 8 m.p.h.), 1955. The smokestack of the Navigation Colliery is just visible in the valley below.

Pack-horse bridge, Aberbeeg, 1960s. This was the old crossing point of the River Ebbw in the area and is over two hundred years old.

The dismantling of the Crumlin Viaduct, 1966. With the closure in 1964 of the Pontypool Road to Neath railway line, which the viaduct had carried over the Ebbw Valley, the days of this magnificent construction were sadly numbered. All that remains today are two stone stumps visible on either side of the valley. In the 1850s the Newport, Abergavenny and Hereford Railway Company commissioned a viaduct at Crumlin to complete a line which would link up with the Taff Vale Railway at Quaker's Yard. This would enable the transport to the Midlands of the valuable iron and coal traffic from Merthyr and Dowlais. The contract went to Thomas Kennard & Sons of Falkirk, Scotland and work began in 1853. The materials used were: 2,400 tons of ironwork (much of which was cast in Falkirk and transported to Crumlin), 30,000 cubic feet of timber and 11,000 cubic feet of masonery. The length of the viaduct was 1,658ft and at its highest point above the valley it measured some 200ft. At the official opening on 1 June 1857 the total cost of the work stood at £62,000 but such was the quality of its construction that the £10,000 spent on repairs in the 1920s appears to be the only sizable additional cost incurred in its life-span of over one hundred years. Thomas Kennard also built himself a house during the project and this later became the Crumlin School of Mines.

Car crash on Cemetry Road from which, mercifully, both driver and passenger walked away, 1980s.

Last train down the valley, Abertillery, 1987. The picture was taken from the Black bridge near the King's Head and shows the train transporting disassembled sections of track down the valley. Following behind the track came a crane which lifted sections of the track onto the flats pulled behind the train. Although passenger service on the line had ceased in 1971 a single track line was maintained in operation for colliery traffic until the closure of Rose Heyworth in 1985 (see p.31).

Three

A Community and its People

Alma Street, Abertillery, c.1900. The street was named after the 1854 battle of Alma in the Crimean War. The terrace on the right was demolished about 1970 as part of a renovation and land reclamation project.

View of Abertillery and the Tillery valley, 1896. The foreground is dominated by the Abertillery Tinworks complex, while on the opposite side of the railway line is Abertillery station with the new Bush Hotel under construction to its right. On the slope immediately

above is Abertillery School (the "British"). In the centre of the picture, to the right of the Tillery river are the Gray and Penybont collieries in full production.

Grandpa and granddaughter
photographed at the studio of J. Cuthbert,
Artist and Photographer, Alma Street,
Abertillery, c.1905.

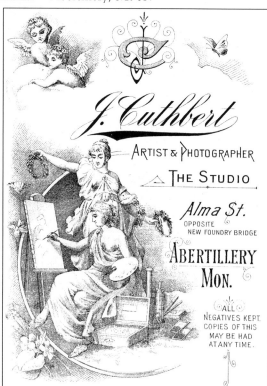

The reverse of the above card
advertising Mr Cuthbert's photographic
studio.

Miss Nellie Francis, later wife of Mr Edgar Bevan (seated centre) with two friends, c.1905. They were all schoolteachers at the "British" School in Abertillery.

The Moore children: George, Gwyn, Bert and Dorothy, Arrail Street, Six Bells, c.1915. At this time professional photographers would often go house-calling in an effort to drum up business. With Mother out he had a relatively easy job persuading the children to pose for the camera.

The bandstand, Abertillery Park, c.1905.

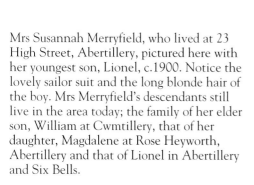

Mrs Susannah Merryfield, who lived at 23 High Street, Abertillery, pictured here with her youngest son, Lionel, c.1900. Notice the lovely sailor suit and the long blonde hair of the boy. Mrs Merryfield's descendants still live in the area today; the family of her elder son, William at Cwmtillery, that of her daughter, Magdalene at Rose Heyworth, Abertillery and that of Lionel in Abertillery and Six Bells.

Postcard of Abertillery post office sent to Private Gor Phillips stationed in Norwich, 1915.

The haunting face of Freda Burnell, c.1920, first victim of Abertillery child murderer, Harold Jones. On 5 February 1921 eight-year old Freda left her house on a errand for her mother to buy chicken food from the Mortimer's pet shop on Somerset Street. Her family never saw her alive again. News of Freda's disappearance soon spread and teams of police and local people scoured the countryside in search of the little girl. Eventually the following morning, her body was found lying in an alleyway off Duke Street, a few hundred yards from her home. Scotland Yard police, called in to help solve the case, soon came to suspect the Mortimers' assistant, fifteen year-old, Harold Jones, of involvement in the murder. He was arrested and stood trial in June at Monmouth Assizes. However, although evidence seemed to mount against him it was dismissed by the defence as circumstantial, and perhaps motivated by disbelief that such a young man could have been capable of this horrific crime, the jury acqitted Jones. He returned to Abertillery, welcomed home by the town band and townsfolk, acutely relieved that it had not been "one of their own."

The grave of Freda Burnell, Brynithel Cemetry, 1980s. Two weeks after his release, eleven year old Florence Little vanished from the street on which Harold Jones lived. Search parties were organised for a second time and house to house calls carried out by police. Attention soon turned to the Jones' home and it was here in the attic that the blood-stained body of the girl was found. An estimated 50,000 people attended the funeral of Florence Little and there were scenes of high emotion as she was laid to rest in Brynithel Cemetry, a short distance from the grave of Freda Burnell. From his prison cell, awaiting a second trial, Harold Jones wrote out separate confessions to the two murders explaining his motivation as "the desire to kill" and producing the chilling revelation that he had quickly to wash the dead girl's blood from his hand and face before answering the door to her mother. In November at Monmouth, Jones pleaded guilty to murder. Three months short of his sixteenth birthday, he cheated the gallows and was sentenced to be detained during His Majesty's pleasure.

The excavation team led by Trevor Lewis, an archaeology student at University College, Aberystwyth, 1924. Between 1924 and 1926 Lewis investigated the site of Castell Taliorum by St Illtyd's Church. Local legend links the area to the Romans and, as a stronghold, the site, dominating the valley below, would have its attractions for any power seeking to subjugate the surrounding inhabitants. However, the Lewis dig found no hard archaeological evidence to support this theory and concluded that the foundations excavated were those of medieval fortified buildings, one cruciform and the other circular in shape. (see map). The sturdiness of the cruciform keep was notable, average thickness of the stone walls being 8-9ft with a total area of 295 square yards. Internal wall space measured 159 square yards, i.e. barely half that of the walls. This disparity is even more marked in the case of the circular building where the area of the walls (268 square yards) was more than three times that of the inside area. The dressed stones found on the site possessed fine ribbed marks. These were identified as the result of a chisel not in use until the twelfth century and are therefore a key clue to the accurate dating of Castell Taliorum. The design of the cruciform building conforms to other Norman keeps built c.1200 and also resembles the cross of a Norman church. The round building, meanwhile, may have been a refuge tower of the type built up to the thirteenth century. In these the doorway was some distance above the ground and the lower stories had small slits instead of windows.

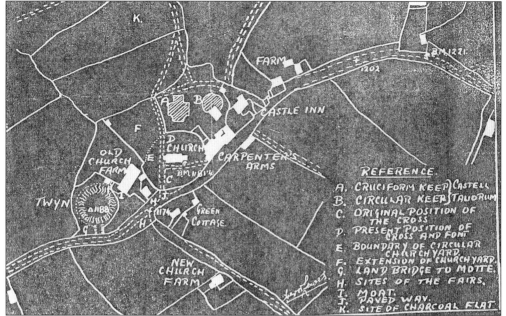

A map drawn up by Trevor Lewis at the conclusion of the dig, 1926, showing the medieval remains in the area. Note the mound to the south-west of the Old Church Farm, clearly visible from the road today. Its origins are uncertain, possibly it was a Norman motte defence connected to the Castell Taliorum site or the grave of an ancient warrior. Legend is as usual far more colourful, claiming the mound was formed by stones dropped from the apron of Ithel, a local giant.

The product of the excavation work at Castell Taliorum, 1924.

Ty-Arthur Farm, Abertillery, c.1925. From left to right, back row: Richard Ireland, Vernon Hughes, Lewis Lewis, Jimmy Arnold. Front row: Joe Lewis (gamekeeper), Bill Price (butcher), Joe Wallace (farmer). Note that a slaughtered pig is hanging in the background; salted, the meat would keep for a considerable time through the winter and in many rural areas formed the basis of inter-farm meals and socialising.

Ty Pwdr farmhouse, Cwmtillery, c.1930. The name of the building translates as "rotten" or "corrupt" house and there may well be a criminal connection with the Rhiw Lladron ("Thieves Slope") track which leads from the nearby Greenmeadow Farm over the mountain to Pontypool.

Ruins of Blaentillery Farm, c.1930

Looking down the Tillery valley from the Gwrhyd Farm, c.1930.

Aberbeeg Square, c.1920, with the Hanbury Hotel in the background.

A view of Aberbeeg Square from 1983 showing the work underway on the construction of the new road, but before the demolition of the row top right. Picture by Pam Hopkins.

Looking north-eastwards from Aberbeeg towards the colliery spoil heap and the village of Six Bells, c.1930. The roof of Aberbeeg Hospital is in the foreground.

The Central Assembly Rooms seen here before they became the first Abertillery headquarters of the Royal British Legion, the organisation founded in 1921 for the assistance of ex-servicemen and women. To the left is the George Inn (W.T. Harvey, proprietor).

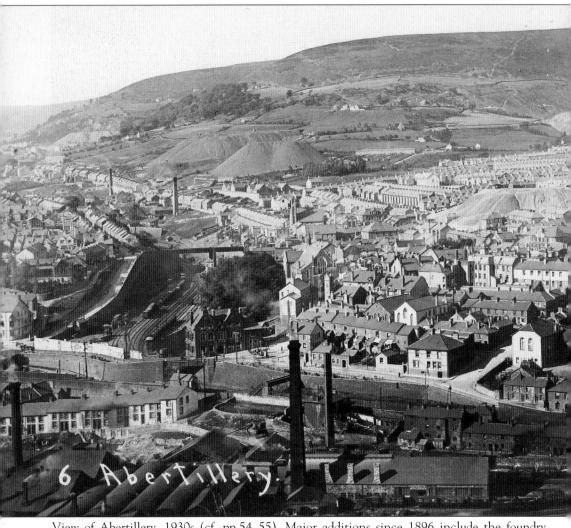

View of Abertillery, 1930s (cf. pp.54–55). Major additions since 1896 include the foundry bridge, the rebuilt St Michael's Church, the Tillery Street Methodist Church and, opposite the Bush Hotel, the post office.

Percy and Albert Williams in the break in the Arael Mountain overlooking Abertillery, 1926. The fault had developed due to subsidence caused by colliery workings below.

Lower Gwastad Terrace, Cwmtillery, c.1930.

Somerset Street, looking north, 1909 with, left, the impressive premises of the Pontlottyn Shop (established 1875), now KwikSave (see p.85).

Somerset Street, Abertillery, c.1937. Woolworths (left of picture), now situated on the High Street, was opened at 39/47 Somerset Street on 24 April 1931 under the management of Mr A. Smith. It was then a 3d and 6d stores with no individual item above the latter price. This "five and dime" store format had first been imported to this country from America in 1909 and was the first in Britain to allow customers to browse and inspect goods on the shelves instead of asking for them over the counter. It was to prove an immediate success. Pre-war advertisements made a point of reassuring customers that 88 per cent of Woolworths goods were British made. It would be interesting to discover what the current percentage is.

The Globe public house, High Street, Abertillery, probably decorated in celebration of V.E. Day, 8 May 1945. Once situated opposite the Midland Bank the site is now part of the main bus stop. The sign above the door tells us that this was one of the houses owned by Webbs Brewery, Aberbeeg.

Queuing for milk at the Cottonwood Cafe (formerly the post office) during the Great Snow of 1947.

Corner of Church Street and High Street during the 1947 snow. G.A. Moxley, tailor and gentleman's mercer of 1 Church Street was a leading figure among the small traders of Abertillery and in 1936 he was the Chairman of Abertillery Shopping Week Committee.

The Prince of Wales Hotel, High Street, Abertillery, viewed from Church Street, c.1950. The Maypole Dairy Co. Ltd, to the left, is now Gus Jones, Jewellers.

Bush Hotel, Abertillery, c.1952, with, in front, the underground public toilets.

Somerset Street, Abertillery, 1960s. The street has since been changed to a one-way system and the pictured car would now be travelling in the wrong direction.

The four Price brothers, Owen, David, Bill and George, on the mountain above Aberbeeg, c.1960. They are pictured after the rescue of George's dog, Jacko, which had fallen down a hole.

Church Street, Abertillery, c.1960, before pedestrianisation. The bus on the left has halted at what was the central stop for Abertillery. This has since moved to the site of the old church school (later Abertillery library) by St Michael's.

Church Street, 1960s, with Abertillery Co-op to the right. On the left, at the far end of Church Street is the Tillery Street Wesleyan Methodist Church. Gutted by a fire in 1980 this distinctive Abertillery landmark is now demolished. The congregation has since worshipped in the annex of the old church, now known as Powell Street Methodists.

View of Abertillery and the Tillery Valley from the "break" on the Arael mountain, 1982.

View of Six Bells and Abertillery, 1983.

Mr Billy Hill from Six Bells, 1993.

Billy Hill and his dog, pictured in 1993, helping out at Dennis Hale's smallholding in Cwm Nant-y-Groes. Earlier in his life Billy farmed both the Ty Dafydd and Gilfach Wen farms and also worked at Blaenserchan Colliery. He moved to Six Bells in 1968. His grandfather had come to area in the 1850s to work on the Crumlin Viaduct and had subsequently built Cross Fence Cottage on Llanhilleth Mountain as his home (see p.29) Billy was born in 1905 and was educated initially at Pantygasseg School where he was taught in Welsh, an indication of how the language still survived at that time in parts of the area. In 1901 one in ten of the population (11.5%) of the population of the Abertillery Urban District was recorded as speaking Welsh. By 1921, however, the figure was down to 3.7% as the language continued to die with those who spoke it.

Hanbury Hotel before its demolition in 1992.

Four
Trade and Industry

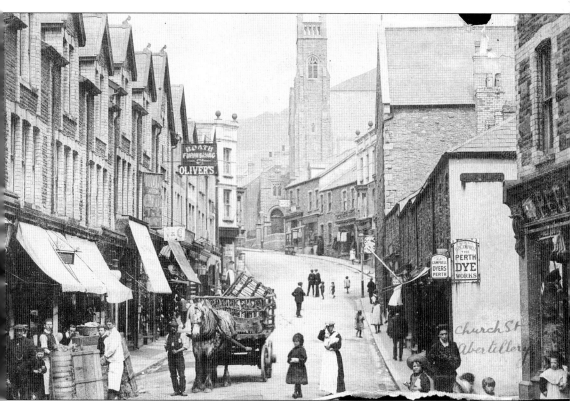

Church Street, c.1910, with three stores well known through south Wales clearly visible: Oliver's, Roath Furnishing and, to the right, Pegler's Stores.

Carpenters Arms, c.1905, known locally as the "Old Church pub" due to its position next to St Illtyd's Church. Note that even the dog has been told to look at the camera. The present landlords are George and Brenda Galloway.

The confectionery shop of S. Moore, Six Bells, 1910s.

Boys pose amongst the rubbish behind the Pontlottyn shop, Abertillery, c.1910. This area was the site of the old market.

The first premises occupied by the Abertillery Bon Marche, Somerset Street, c.1900.

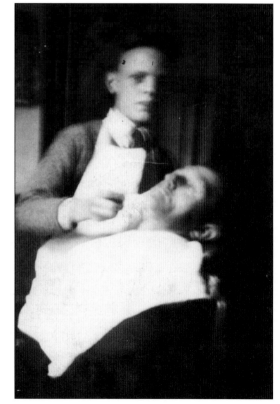

Lather boy, Arthur Lewis, 1930s. He later went on to become manager of the Six Bells Colliery. Recently, he was awarded the O.B.E. largely for his work throughout the world with BESO (British Executive Service Overseas).

"232"
GREY FLANNELS

PUBLIC favour is not lightly bestowed. Success comes to products which deserve it. Only a high standard of quality and out-of-the-ordinary value could win the popularity which has been gained and is maintained by "232" Flannels.

"232" Flannels have set a new standard of merit which is still strides ahead of the next best. That standard will never be lowered.

The range of "232" Flannels includes the famous cloth in four shades, Light, Dark, Silver-tone and **14/11** Silver Ash ....

BON MARCHE LTD.,
ABERTILLERY.
'BUS AND TRAIN FARES PAID AS USUAL.

Bon Marche Ltd advertisement from the 1930s. This was then Monmouthshire's largest store.

As this and the advertisement opposite reveal Bon Marche and the Pontlottyn Shop were in intense competition for dominance of the Abertillery area clothing market. Both pages are taken from the official programme advertising the third Abertillery and District Chamber of Trade Empire Shopping Week held between 3 and 10 October 1931, when with the local economy still losing the battle with Depression all retailers were desperate to attract what disposable income remained in the district.

PONTLOTTYN SHOP

THE WESTERN VALLEY'S PREMIER STORE.

THE LEADING

Fashion Centre

of Abertillery & Western Valleys.

Always First with Fashion's Latest Decree

COMBINED WITH BEST VALUE AND SERVICE.

Your Inspection of our **NEW AUTUMN GOODS** is invited.

Tel. 68. **MORGAN & FRANCIS** B. Francis, Proprietor.

Advertisement for the Pontlottyn Shop, 1931. The clocking on machine used by employees at this time is now on display at Abertillery Museum.

"PAROMALT"

The *Ucal* Brand of

PARRISH'S FOOD
COD LIVER OIL
AND
MALT EXTRACT

makes little bodies STRONG —and big bodies STRONGER

PRICES

1lb	1'6
2lb	2'9

A Child's Food and Tonic Combined

contains valuable flesh-and-bone-forming properties.

A POWERFUL DIGESTIVE AGENT & NERVE TONIC.

Go to PRICHARD'S

For all your "U.C.A.L." Goods
—and for Safe and Efficient **N.H.I.** DISPENSING.

MEDICAL HALL,
CHURCH STREET,
CAMERA HOUSE, **ABERTILLERY.** BLAINA, CARDIFF, MERTHYR, &c.

Advertisement from 1936 for the still marvellous cod-liver oil, thankfully now available in the more palatable capsule form.

The window of John Jones, butcher's of Commercial Street, Abertillery dressed spectacularly for the *Daily Express* National Shop Window Display Competition, 1930s. Mr Jones' son, Hercules ("Erky") later took over the shop.

The entry of T.H. Prichard & Son, Ltd, chemists of 48 Church Street, Abertillery in the Daily Mail's Show and Sell Contest, 1930s. First settling in Abertillery in 1893, by 1905 Thomas Prichard had four premises: at the Medical Hall and at Church Street, Abertillery, High Street, Blaina and Hanbury Road, Bargoed. In 1926 he retired to Weston-Super-Mare. To commemorate the event the Ebenezer Baptist Church held a social evening in which Mr Prichard was presented with an illuminated address as a mark of the high esteem in which he was held by his fellow worshippers. A staunch non-conformist and total abstainer, Prichard had held the positions of deacon, Honorary Secretary, trustee, Sunday School teacher, President of the Monmouthshire Baptist Association (1912-13), councillor and in 1911-12, chairman of Abertillery Urban District Council. As a small businessman whose work was underpinned by a strong Christian faith and sense of public duty, Prichard was typical of the men who were influential in the town's affairs during the late nineteenth and early twentieth century.

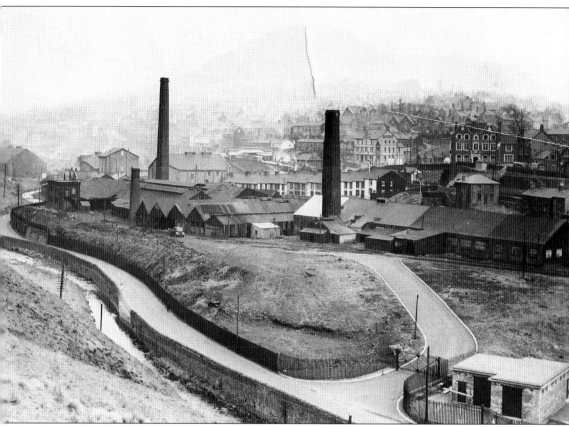

Abertillery Tinworks, c.1950. The original tinworks on the site was founded in 1846 by Mr J. Pearce and Mr John Conway. In the 1851 census Conway is listed as a magistrate and tinplate manufacturer, aged 44 and living at No.8, Cwmtillery. Known locally as "the Works", the business finally closed in 1957 after 111 years in operation. 400 jobs were lost.

"Warwill"

FOUNDRY and ENGINEERING WORKS
ABERTILLERY

Manufacturers of **CASTINGS** (in iron and brass) for Collieries, Tinplate and Steel Works, Councils and Contractors.

GENERAL ENGINEERS

WORKMANSHIP & ACCURACY
guaranteed.

Specializing in the manufacture of Tinning and Cleaning Plant for Tinplate Works. Machine cut gears (in iron, steel and non-ferrous metals) up to 4' 6" diameter, Spurs, Spirals, Worms, Worm Wheels, Chain Wheel Sprockets. Complete Drives designed and supplied.

Telephone 71.   *Telegrams: " WARWILL."*

Advertisement for Warwill's Foundry and Engineering Works dating from the 1930s.

Revd Llywelyn Williams M.P. for Abertillery (1950–65) talking to men at the entrance to the tinworks.

Chivers & Sons brewery, Crook Hill, Cwmtillery, 1970s.

OLD "TOG"
IS NOW AT
The "BELL."

"It's better to drink
And then feel bad,
Than not to drink,
And wish you had."

PHONE 144.

SOMERSET STREET
— AND —
MARKET STREET,
ABERTILLERY

UPSIDE DOWN . . . as Usual!

Advertisement for The Bell public house, Abertillery, 1931. Known as the Top and Bottom Bell, with its two entrances onto both Market Street and Somerset Street, it provided an ideal haunt for crafty under age drinkers who had the choice of two escape routes to evade the inquiries of a passing policeman.

91

The Man who Drinks

WEBB'S

ABERBEEG

BEERS

One Smile is Worth a Thousand Frowns in any Market————————SO SMILE !

Webb's brewery advertisement, 1936. This brewery was established in Aberbeeg in 1837 and remained in operation until the 1980s when production was transferred to Ebbw Vale by Welsh Brewers.

A fully operational Webb's Brewery pictured in the early 1970s by Raymond Hawkins, photographer of King Street, Abertillery, who was well known for his aerial views. The houses, bottom left were occupied by brewery personnel such as the chief brewer and the managing director.

Webbs Brewery, 1960s. Picture by Pam Hopkins.

Advertisement for S.M. Ash & Son, 1934.

Mr Emmanuel outside the shop of S.M. Ash, High Street, Abertillery, 1950. On 1 January 1900 Sidney Mortimer Ash opened a saddlers and leather factor's shop in Oak Street, Abertillery and was soon joined in the business by his two sons, Robert and Trevor. As the business grew, Mr Ash moved to larger premises in the block between the Arcade and High Street and a branch was also opened in Blaina. The Abertillery shop is now run by S.M. Ash's grandson, Desmond with his wife, Patricia and children, Robert and Elizabeth. With ninety-five years of continuous activity Ash's is now the oldest surviving family business in Abertillery and the millenium will, it is to be hoped, witness a double celebration for all the family.

Five

The Strength of
Religion

Wesleyan Methodist Church, Llanhilleth, c.1910.

Laying the foundation stone at the Tillery Street Wesleyan Methodist Church, Abertillery, 1906. The last great non-conformist religious revival, which, through the charismatic inspiration of Revd Evan Roberts, swept south Wales in 1905–6, led to the construction of many new chapels and the enlargement of existing buildings. During the constuction of their new church the Wesleyan Methodist congregation held its services at the nearby gymnasium hall in the Institute on Division Street.

Sunday school class, Bethany Methodist Chapel, Six Bells, c.1915.

Tabernacle Congregational Chapel, Chapel Street, Abertillery, 1920s. In the centre is Robert Hall, Choirmaster, Treasurer and life deacon of the chapel.

Chapel Whitsun walk, Abertillery, 1920s.

Abertillery's Plight.

Appeal to the Government.

Full Text of Letter from Ministers and Clergy.

The following is the full text of the letter sent by the ministers and clergy of Abertillery to the Prime Minister, Ministers of Health and Labour, Mr. Ramsay Macdonald, M.P., Mr. Lloyd George, M.P., and Mr. G. Barker, M.P.

ABERTILLERY, Mon.

5th July, 1928.

Sir,

For a considerable time, we, the ministers, and clergy of Abertillery, have been anxiously concerned with the dire necessity of a large section of the people to whom we minister.

We realise that the situation is a very complex one and the result of the action and reaction of forces and conditions operating and extending far beyond the boundaries of our own ministry, and we are aware of the current and often conflicting opinion obtaining with regard to the contributory causes of the sad social and economic conditions of this and other necessitous areas. We do not wish to mention or to discuss these causes.

We are convinced that the root of the evil is to be found in the general disregard of the Christian ethic, and that nothing is more urgently needed than the general realisation of the imperative necessity of good will, mutual respect and Christian co-operation.

We therefore earnestly hope that this letter will contribute to that end and respectfully beg for your patient and sympathetic consideration of the following observations and suggestions.

We view with grave concern and increasing anxiety the conditions prevailing in this area. We would respectfully point out that three of the pits in the locality which gave employment to about 2,500 men have been idle almost continuously for the past three years. Of these the large majority have exhausted their savings. The number of men receiving unemployment benefit at present is about 3,500. A very large proportion of these, as well as the aged, the sick, and widows who are dependent upon poor law relief, are living on the fringe of dire poverty, and we are convinced that nothing short of Government intervention can adequately meet the situation.

We welcome the overseas settlement proposals but would point out that while the policy of migration does assist the individual it yet tends to aggravate the condition for those remaining in this area, because the great burdens of the present debts and the current rate have to be borne by a decreasing population.

The Abertillery Urban District Council has borrowed, as you know, about £80,000 for the purpose of finding work for the unemployed. Again, it owes approximately another £103,000 which it is unable to collect. So heavy is the debt that it is estimated that it takes £200 per week to pay the interest.

Moreover, we understand that Abertillery's share of the debt incurred by the Abertillery and District Water Board is about £300,000, and of that incurred by the Bedwellty Board of Guardians approximately £230,000, making a total of about £713,000. This has to be borne by a population of about 26,290 in an area where the assessable value has decreased by £40,488 in seven years (in 1920 it was £156,049; in 1927 it was £115,561.) The rate in the same period has increased 136 per cent.

It is said that the dire necessity of the people has been exploited for political purposes, and also callously subordinated to political and financial considerations. We desire to emphasise the human aspect, and to point out that the weeds of revolutionary doctrine can thrive easily in the hearts of men embittered by unemployment, continual want, high rents and crushing debts.

For the accumulation of debt we are of the opinion that His Majesty's Government is not without its responsibility. The Government consented to the loans, decided their conditions, and after investigation were apparently satisfied as to the need. If they were unnecessary and unjustifiable the Government might have exercised control over local expenditure at an earlier date. The situation now is so serious and the impoverishment of the people so general and acute that we are convinced that the area not only cannot recover 'a measure of prosperity without substantial Government aid, but also that such aid is needed immediately.

We do not presume to suggest the form which such assistance should take, but we would respectfully suggest that it should be designed :—

(1) To secure a substantial and immediate reduction in the local rates and consequently in the prevailing high rents. Many cases have come to our notice where the rent of the house exceeds 50 per cent. of the occupier's income, while the following facts indicate the destitution :—

Family	Rent	Income	Weekly sum available for food, clothing and lighting	
			Whole family	Per head
	s. d.	s. d.	s. d.	s. d.
Widow and 6 children ...	15 0	36 0	21 0	3 0
Parents and 2 children ...	9 11½	23 0	13 0½	3 3
Parents and 1 child ...	13 8	24 0	10 4	3 5½
Husband and wife	8 0	17 6	9 6	4 9
Man (unemployed)	4 6	10 0	5 6	5 6
Old Age Pensioner & wife	5 0	10 0	,7 0	2 6

(2) To secure the extension of the Old Age Pension Act to include at 65 the wife of the old age pensioner.

(3) To provide schemes of relief work.

(4) To establish subsidiary industries.

(5) To provide for afforestation. The hill-sides, which were well wooded before the war, are now bare.

It is after careful and anxious deliberation that we venture to present the above observations and suggestions, of which we respectfully and earnestly appeal for your earliest and sympathetic consideration.

We are,
Yours respectfully,
(Signed)

J. H. CRETNEY, P.M. Minister.
D. G. JENKINS, Presbyterian Minister.
A. S. LEYLAND, P.M. Minister.
T. REEVES, Baptist Minister.
A. K. SHREWSBURY, Vicar of Six Bells.
W. J. THOMAS, Presbyterian Minister.
T. F. WILLIAMS, Roman Catholic Priest.
DAVID J. WILLIAMS, Wesleyan Minister.
W. L. HARRIS, Vicar of Abertillery (chairman.)
IVOR EVANS, Baptist Minister (secretary.)

" Ty Bryn,"
Blaenau Gwent,

The concern of local ministers for the future of their community is evident from this powerful letter, 1928.

Glandwr Baptist Chapel with, on the hillside in the distance, Christchurch, Llanhilleth, 1920s. The Baptist chapel at Glandwr was founded in 1838 although the congregation there dates from c.1820. In 1906 the building was substantially enlarged into the existing structure.

Whit Sunday walk by the Forward Movement of the Presbyterian Church of Wales, Six Bells, c.1925. From left to right in the front row are the church deacons: Theophilus Watkin Evans (headmaster of Aberbeeg and Gellicrug schools), Henry Edwards, Lewis Morgan. Behind them, standing sideways to the camera, is Charles Phillips (conductor). The Presbyterian Church in Six Bells was built in 1906 and closed in the late 1960s.

The wedding photograph of Mr Worthy Richardson (headmaster of Bryngwyn School) and his new wife, 1920s.

Chapel walk by the Somerset Street Primitive Methodists ("the Prims"), Whit Sunday, 1930.

St Illtyd's Church, near Brynithel, 1920s. It is the oldest building in north-west Gwent dating from the late twelfth century when it was constructed by Cistercian monks farming sheep in the area. However, as a centre of religious worship the site is much older than this and was possibly in use even before the Age of Saints brought Christianity to Wales in the sixth century A.D. The circular churchyard certainly indicates a pre-Norman construction and the existing stone font may well have been part of this earlier building.

Interior shot of nave and chancel at St Illtyd's, 1924. Note the beginnings of decay near the tie beam. In 1957 the church, already in poor state of repair and suffering from diminishing attendances, was closed due to nearby opencast coal working (see p.29) However, although this work finished in 1962 the Church in Wales saw little point in a re-opening and St Illtyd's was permanently closed. Fortunately, through the determination of local people and the sponsorship of the Blaenau Gwent Borough Council and Cadw, the future of the deconsecrated and deteriorating church has since been secured by a comprehensive renovation programme.

The bells of St Illtyd's photographed here in 1993. The bell to the left, presented to the church by the Andrews family, bears the inscription, "Come Away Make No Delay", which traditionally has been thought to refer to a sermon preached there by John Wesley in the eighteenth century. The other bell is inscribed with "Gloria In Excelsis Deo".

St Paul's Anglican Church, Cwmtillery, 1947. This building was constructed between 1888 and 1891 at a cost of £1,100. From 1892 until 1923 when it attained parish status for Cwmtillery, it was a daughter church of St Michael's, Abertillery. St Paul's was built on land donated by the South Wales Colliery Company and it was rumoured that the "new" church bell had previously been in the employ of Cwmtillery Colliery before the steam hooter was installed. Built in the early English Gothic style the church accomodated about 300 worshippers; its external walls were comprised of red sandstone from Gilwern quarries with stone tracery from the Forest of Dean. The bell is now part of the collection at Abertillery Museum.

A vast crowd of mourners looks on at the funeral of Ivor, Reg and Bill, the three sons of the founder of the well-known local bus company, Webb Jones, Aberbeeg Methodist Chapel, 1950. They were victims of the air disaster of 12 March 1950. This was caused when a plane returning supporters from the Ireland-Wales rugby international in Dublin crashed while coming into land at Llandough airfield in the Vale of Glamorgan. Ray Francis of the Prince of Wales public house in Abertillery was also killed in the disaster.

Whit Sunday walk by the Blaenau Gwent Baptist Chapel, outside the Crown pub, Blaenau Gwent, 1952. Most of the chidren seen here would have been pupils of Blaenau Gwent Infants and Cwmtillery Junior schools while the man to the right of the first group is Mr Cyril Lane, a highly respected and well-loved teacher at Cwmtillery Junior School and long-time member of Blaenau Gwent Baptist Chapel.

Blaenau Gwent Baptist Chapel walk, Whit Sunday, c.1960, viewed passing the Liberal Club, Division Street after crossing the Foundry bridge.

The 1906 Blaenau Gwent Baptist Chapel viewed here in the late 1980s shortly before decay in the stonework forced its demolition and replacement by a new church. The first chapel at Blaenau Gwent was built in 1715 although the cause was some fifty years older having been started in the 1660s. The building acted as the major centre of non-conformist worship for the western valleys of Monmouthshire throughout the eighteenth century and well into the nineteenth.

Christchurch, Llanhilleth, 1983. It was erected in 1910 at a cost of £6,000. The first minister was the Revd David Felix.

Six

Education

Class 1B at Blaenau Gwent Infants School, c.1910.

Boys playing marbles at Abertillery Boys School, c.1895. The girls school here was not built until 1898.

Morning exercise drill at the Abertillery Boys School (the "British" School), pre-1903 as the extension on the Alma Street side has not yet been built.

Head teachers and staff at the "British School", c.1915. In the centre of the second row, from left to right: Miss Esther Davies (Head of the Girls School), Mr A.J.(Bertie) Bevan (Head of Boys School and son of the first headmaster, Thomas Bevan who had run the school for 46 years from the early days in the vestry of Blaenau Gwent Baptist Chapel until 1899) and Miss Hiley (Head of Abertillery Infants School).

"Swiss" dancing at Gellicrug School, 1936.

Pupils at the "British School", 1937 with the headmaster, Mr Lawford (left) and their teacher, Mr J.V. Thomas (right).

Cwmtillery Junior School, affectionately known as "the Cock and Chick", 1920s.

Pupils from Bryngwyn School at their sports day in Abertillery Park, c.1955. From left to right, back row: Mr Jim Mounter, Keith Dykes, John Fletcher, -?-, Jeff Jones, George Brewer, Nigel Smith, John Hooper, -?-, Don Bearcroft, Mr M. James. Second row: Jean MacDonald, Chris Brickle, Barbara Tetley, Ceinwen Hill, Jennifer Evans, Wendy Hall, Carol Brooks, Val Holland. Front row: Diane Gough, Jacky Morgan, Diane Gilson, Barbara Edwards, Pam Martin, Elaine Winters, Pam Beach.

Nativity celebration at Blaenau Gwent Infants School, c.1955.

Abertillery County (Grammar) School, 1959. From left to right, back row: Deri Jones, Geoffrey Drake, David Pike, John Brown, Elwyn Griffiths, Terry Winmill, Jeffrey Hurley. Second row: Jillian Glissett, Peggy Lambert, Lesley Jackson, Diane Berrow, Margaret Meredith, Ann Rees, Rosalind Price. Front row: Elizabeth Lewis, Ann Humphries, Angela Ford, Valerie Sweet, Valerie Davies, Janet Venn, Mary Soffe, Margaret Sheean, Hirell Watkins.

The "British School", c.1960.

Queen Street Junior School, c.1972.

St David's Day celebrations at Blaenau Gwent Infants School, affectionately known as the "Crown School" after the nearby pub, c.1975. Picture by Pam Hopkins.

Pupils from Ty'r Graig School, Aberbeeg, many of whom are the children and grandchildren of men who worked in the local mines, discover their mining heritage during a visit to Big Pit, Blaenavon, 1986. From left to right, back row: Steffan Meek, Dean Jones, Mrs Dyer, Kathryn Burge, Mrs Crockett, Chanine Tovey, Emma Robinson. Middle row: David Richardson, Tanya Mitchell, Natalie Green, Nathan Warren, Greg Tovey, Dafydd Edwards, Jason Mann, Lee Poulsom. Front row (sic): Karen Deacon, James Chivers, Sarah Hopkins.

Abertillery Primary School better known as the "British School" pictured shortly before its closure in 1987 after 138 years of service to the community. It had been founded in 1849 by the British and Foreign Bible Society from whom it took its name. The site is now occupied by the Cwrt Mytton home for the elderly, named after Cllr T.H. Mytton J.P. (Chairman of Abertillery U.D.C. in 1924-25 and 1934, and for many years a prime mover in the affairs of the town).

Seven

Service to the Community

Abertillery fire brigade, c.1925.

British soldiers pose with the ambulance donated by the people of Abertillery for use in the First World War.

Troops on parade in Abertillery Park before the unveiling of Abertillery War Memorial, 1920.

Abertillery War Memorial, 1920.

Mr Gulliford, first caretaker of Powell's Tillery Workmen's Institute opened in Division Street, Abertillery in 1898.

Abertillery fire engine serving here as a hearse for the funeral of one of the members of the brigade, Alexandra Road, Six Bells, 1920s. Note the Union Jack draped around the coffin.

Advertisement for the 1931 eisteddfod which aimed to raise funds for the upkeep of Abertillery and District Hospital, Aberbeeg.

Abertillery and District Hospital, Aberbeeg, c.1965. The hospital was officially opened on 30 September 1922 by Cllr Thomas H. Mytton (Chairman of Abertillery and District Hospital Committee 1916-22) on land given by the Hanbury Estate. The total cost of the finished building was ú76,000 almost entirely raised by voluntary contributions from the workers of the Abertillery area. This helps explain the pride that local people have always taken in "their" hospital and their legitimate concerns for its future. Initially, 44 beds were available and, briefly, during the 1920s, the hospital housed one of the first Marie Stopes birth control clinics in the country. Picture by Pam Hopkins.

ABERTILLERY & DISTRICT HOSPITAl

SECOND ANNUAL

Eisteddfod

SATURDAY, SEPT. 26th,

1931, to be held at the

Trinity and Wesleyan Churches, Abertillery.

MALE VOICE & GIRL GUIDES' CHOIR COMPETITIONS, EXCELLENT VOCAL, INSTRUMENTAL, ELOCUTION, LITERARY, ART, & NEEDLEWORK COMPETITIONS.

ENJOY THIS MUSICAL TREAT AND

Help Our Hospital.

PROGRAMMES, post free 2½d., from the Eisteddfod Secretary, T. ELLIS ROWLANDS, 31 Evelyn Street, Abertillery.

Admission : 1/-   CHILDREN under 16 HALF-PRICE.

Abertillery and District Water Board, 1935–36, pictured at the Grwyne Fawr reservoir. From left to right, back row: Cllr H.T. Williams, W. Tolson (Deputy Accountant), R. Williams, Cllr A.E. Jones, W. Revill (Works Inspector), Cllr J.E. Day. Front row: Cllr E.J. Lewis, Cllr I. Morgan, I. Holland (Reservoir Keeper), W. Cory Goddard M.I.C.E. (Acting Engineer), Cllr F. Hayes, J.P., H. Horton Tolson, J.P. (Accountant and Registrar), Cllr W.J. Lawrence, Cllr W. Beynon, Cllr T. Gale (Chairman), Cllr P.W. Williams, Cllr S. Garland, J.P. (Vice-Chairman), N.C. Moses (Deputy Solicitor). The group contains many men prominent in the public life of Abertillery; Cllrs Day (1939–40), Hayes (1935 and 1935–36), Beynon (1929–30 and 1936–37) and Gale (1931–32 and 1947–48) were all chairmen of Abertillery Urban District Council. By the end of the last century it had become apparent that the rapidly growing demand for water in Abertillery and the booming Western Valleys of Monmouthshire could not be met by the locally available supply. The remarkable struggle for sufficent water, however, proved to be a protracted one, due largely to the logistical nightmare of transporting water from the designated reservoir site some 22 miles away in the heart of the Black Mountains. Here the water would be stored at approximately 1,800ft above sea level, a height which allowed a gravity feed down to any point of the Board's area (the urban districts of Abertillery, Abercarn, Mynyddislwyn and Risca). At Abertillery the draw-off level was to be 1,150 ft and at Risca a mere 200ft. The first surveys were carried out in the isolated Grwyne Fawr Valley in 1906 but it was not until 3 August 1910 that the Act of Parliament to incorporate the Abertillery and District Water Board received Royal Assent. The contract for the construction of the reservoir was secured the following year by William Underwood & Brother of Dukinfield, Cheshire. In 1915 it was agreed to suspend work for the duration of the war and it was not until 1919 that the Board, now responsible for the construction after the release of Underwood from the contract, restarted work. Such was the scale of the task and the isolation of the Grwyne Fawr site that a navvy village was erected out of nothing further down the valley at Blaen-y-cwm to house the hundreds of labourers, stonemasons and craftsmen needed for the job. In 1925 over 400 people were reported living in this "frontier" settlement with 49 children attending the day school. On 28 March 1928 the reservoir was finally opened at an estimated final cost of £1 million. With the project complete the village was demolished and the specially-built supply railway pulled up.

Grwyne Fawr reservoir, Black Mountains, 1993. Its capacity is approximately 400 million gallons.

Funeral procession of long-serving Salvation Army bandmaster, Albert Veal, Abertillery, 1935. The "Sally Army" was active in Abertillery from the last nineteenth century and its Founder-General, William Booth (1829–1912) preached to large crowds during his visits to the town in 1907 and 1909.

Juanito Enrique and Germinal Garcia, two of the Basque refugee children given sanctuary in the area during the Spanish Civil War (1936–39). The conflict was played out between the forces of the Republic (communist/socialist) and the Nationalists (fascists) under General Franco. It captured the imagination of many young men in south Wales, an area which had become home to many working class Spanish immigrants and had forged close links with the industrialised Basque Country of Spain. A total of 174 Welsh volunteers, the great majority communist miners, enlisted in the honourable cause of the International Brigade. Thirty-three of them were never to return. In an example of great humanity, and despite the continuing economic crisis which ground on in the south Wales coalfield, lodges managed to raise funds, food and clothing were gathered for the people of the Spanish Republic, and refugees cared for.

Joe Meredith of 47 Attlee Court, Abertillery pictured here (left) as a 19 year old soldier in "D" Company, 2nd Battalion, Middlesex Regiment, loading mortars on the banks of the river Rhein just above Dusseldorf, February 1945. Joe had earlier been one of the first soldiers to land on the Normandy beaches during the D Day invasion of June 1944. In a remarkable chance event Joe's wife was to come across the picture when the page of the *South Wales Argus* in which it appeared was used to wrap bread she had bought in Glandwr Street.

A.R.P. (Air Raid Precautions)
training exercise, Abertillery, 1940.

Women's Voluntary Service, Abertillery, 1940s. The W.V.S., formed in 1938, performed
sterling support work during the Second World War.

Committee organised as part of the Ministry of Food's efforts to improve the nutrition and health of children in post-war Britain, Ebenezer Chapel, Abertillery, c.1953. In his chain of office is Billy Derrick, Chair of Abertillery Urban District Council (1953–54). He is holding a bottle of cod liver oil, which, along with orange juice and dried milk, the Government was seeking to promote.

Visit to Aberbeeg Hospital in 1958 of Mrs Vijaya Pandit, Indian High Commissioner to the U.K. (1955–61). She was the sister of Nehru, the first prime minister of independent India.

Abertillery and District Hospital fete, 1959.

Abertillery Urban District Council, 1960–61, chaired by Cllr Stan Butler.

Abertillery Sea Cadet Corps working on the construction of a new parade ground in front of their Lancaster Street headquarters, Six Bells, c.1955. The boat behind the boys was their practice vessel, a 27ft cutter. After reaching a dilapidated state the boat, as M.O.D. property, was burnt according to Navy regulations. First formed in 1943 several hundred young men were trained as cadets under the guidance of the commanding officer, Evan Watkins, until the disbanding of the unit in the early 1960s.

The opening of Brynithel Community Centre, 1965. From left to right, at the back standing in the doorway: Ray Taylor, Towi Berrow, Cllr Idris Pope B.E.M., J.P.(Chairman of Abertillery U.D.C. 1946–47 and 1954–55, Mayor of Blaenau Gwent 1974–75, Freeman of the Borough of Blaenau Gwent from 1978). Front row: Harry Lewis (Clerk of the Council), Emrys Davies (Welfare Officer C.I.S.W.O.), Cllr John Thomas (Chairman of Abertillery U.D.C. 1965–66), Emlyn Williams (President N.U.M.), Cliff Lane, Alderman Frank Whatley (Monmouthshire County Council), Phillip Maggs, Dai Francis (Secretary N.U.M.). Picture by Pam Hopkins.

Firemen inside the gutted interior of the Walpole Hotel, Llanhilleth, now the rugby club, c.1956. Up the ladder is Lyn Watkins watched by Bernard Mahoney, both members of Abertillery Fire Brigade. The call was received at 5.30 in the morning and the Abertillery boys arrived shortly afterwards. Rumour has it that Lyn (known to like his drink), hearing that a "watering hole" was in danger, got there a good five minutes before the rest!

Webbs brewery delivery men, Bill Prestig (far left) and Paddy Hucker are congratulated at the Hanbury Hotel by fellow workers and management in the Hanbury Hotel after their quick thinking and bravery resulted in the rescue of two children from a housefire in Cwm, 1970. Bill (a part-time fireman) and Paddy were each presented with a canteen of cutlery by the brewery. The "toasters" from left to right: Aubrey Jones (managing director), Robert Hemms, Graham Davies, Ron Kimber, Phillip Lewis, Russel Morgan, Mike Stowmark, Don Rees (depot manager).

Community policeman, Chris Arnold of 33 Bryngwyn Road, Six Bells seen here, c.1985, presenting Mrs Rita Evans, Matron of Aberbeeg Hospital, with the proceeds of a sponsored penalty shoot-out. This was held between schools in the area in order to raise funds for the hospital. In 1991 P.C. Arnold was awarded the B.E.M. (the British Empire Medal, now replaced by the M.B.E.) for his services to the community. Chris is a schools liaison and crime prevention officer for the local police force, a past President of Abertillery Lions Club, a youth club worker and coach for the Abertillery Junior School football team.

Eight
"A Really Good Time Together"

The annual ox-roast held at the end of Division Street, Abertillery, c.1925. Division Street was so named as it marked the old boundary between Abertillery and Cwmtillery.

Charabanc trip from Abertillery to Somerset, 1923. Notice the solid tyres which must have made for a bone-shaking ride at times.

A tiger, obviously long since stuffed, provides a novel photographic prop for this studio. The card's message reads: "Dear Father, I am coming down to see you soon, but not on this one. From Wyn."

Before the mass availability of television changed leisure habits four cinemas flourished alongside each other in the centre of Abertillery. The Empress (a site now occupied by the bottom Lymes Club) and the Pavilion cinemas were both on Carlyle Sreet, the Gaiety on Bridge Street and the Palace where the snooker club now stands on Camel Street.

Six Bells lido (open air swimming pool), 1935. This was built by unemployed men and funded by voluntary contributions of 1d a week.

Carnival Queen and her court, Six Bells, 1951.

Celebrations in Blenheim Street, Six Bells, viewed from Llwyn-on Road, 1940s. The van behind the group was the Morris 8 (Series E) belonging to Bert Tunadine's bakery.

Coronation tea party at the back of Blaenau Gwent rows, 1953. These five terraces each consisted of 13 houses and were intended as accommodation for workers at the Rose Heyworth Colliery. Built on fields lying between Glyn Mawr Uchaf and Glyn Mawr Canol farms they were hence originally known as the Glynmawr Cottages or Newtown. They were opened on 1 August 1874 with impressive ceremony perhaps due to the fact that Colonel Heyworth himself was responsible for much of the exterior architecture as well as the design, inside, of a new more economical fire grate.

Festival of Britain celebrations, Abertillery, 1951. From left to right, back row: Pat Lucas (with shawl), -?-, Anita Morris, Doreen Cooper, Peggy Lambert, Pamela Williams. Front row: Mary Lambert, Mary Evans, Diane Hares, Gillian Morris, Ann Owen.

Coronation street party, High Street, Six Bells, 1953.

Waiting for the Carnival to arrive, Cwm Cottage Road, Abertillery, 1950s. Visible far left is the corner of the Drill Hall.

Arrail Street party, Six Bells, held to celebrate the Investiture of Prince Charles as Prince of Wales, 1969. Kneeling in the foreground by her daughter, Kathryn, is Lilian Butler. Picture by Pam Hopkins.

Rediffusion staff outing to Bristol Zoo, June 1954.

Woodland Terrace, Aberbeeg, celebrating the Investiture of Prince Charles, 1969. The scene includes many people well known in the Aberbeeg area. Seated in the foreground (right) are Mr and Mrs Howard Collins who ran the Hanbury Hotel for many years. Mrs Collins now lives at Grace Pope Court, Llanhilleth. Standing in the gateway of the building to the right, then the local police station, is Mrs Cook, who, with her husband, Cliff ran the village shop. Cliff operated one of the first mobile shops in the area. The Robinson family is also well represented

with Mr Ralph Robinson, his brother Norman, Mrs Hazel Robinson, the local postmistress, and her daughter, Ann (in the spotted dress and black hat). Left of picture in front of the doorway of Anne's Wool Shop is Mr Herbert William Pennell, organist at Christchurch for 65 (!!) years from 1909 to 1974. Also in the picture are his daughter, Edna Bailey, his son-in-law, Phillip and his granddaughter, Christine (now a teacher in Abertillery Primary). Picture by Pam Hopkins.

Six Bells women's football team, Prince of Wales' Investiture celebrations, 1969.

Bert and Dorothy Snellgrove watching a Six Bells street party held to celebrate the Silver Jubilee of Elizabeth II, 1977.

Nine
Song and Performance

Abertillery Salvation Army band, 1908.

Arael Griffin Colliery Brass Band, c.1900.

Phyllis Bevan, daughter of the head master of the "British" School, dressed as a Dutch girl for the production of *Jan of Windmill Land*, c.1916.

Ebenezer Revival Mission Band, Abertillery, 1905. From left to right, back row: George Malsom, T. Powell, W. Randel, W. Morgan, W.G. Richards. Fourth row: George Waters (Vice-President), W. James, J. Bridgewater, J.T.H. Davies, E. Cuff, W. Stanfield, Dl. Hayward, H. Wheeler. Third row: Mrs Mudway, Mrs Morgan, Mrs Meek, R. Byard, D. Lewis, W. Mudway, Mrs Lewis, J. Williams (Visiting Secretary), J. Davies. Second row: Mrs Powell, Mrs Bridgewater, Mrs Cuff, Tom James, Revd D. Collier (Pastor), W. Lewis (President of the band, and also Chairman of Abertillery Urban District Council, 1902–03), Mrs Davies, Mrs Hayward, Mrs Hawkins, Mrs Pope. Front row: W. Skinner, Miss L. Owen, W. Meek (Secretary), Miss A. Oldland, E. King.

The Philharmonic Gleemen photographed outside St Michael's Vicarage, October 1945.

Ron Jones (buses) starring as the Major General Stanley in Abertillery Operatic Society's production of Gilbert & Sullivan's *The Pirates of Penzance*, 1951.

The performance of *Magyar Melody* by the Abertillery Amateur Dramatic and Musical Society (aka the Operatic Society), 1957. The society's first production was *The Mikado* performed at the Metropole Theatre and Opera House, Abertillery in 1916. The first musical director was Mr M.E. Thomas (1916–17) followed by Mr Luther Evans (1918–39), Mr Cyril Blake (1951), Mr Maurice David (1952–1976), Mr Derek Jenkins (1977–1982), Mrs Joyce Jones (1983–1991), Mrs Joy Catley (1992) and Mr Dennis Hutchins (1993–present). The producers since 1957 have been Jack and Melba Wells. In November 1962 the society was joint winner of the N.C.B. Light Opera Competition with its first venture into the world of modern musicals – *Oklahoma*. This success was continued the following year with a second place for their production of *Showboat*. As well as annual musicals in October the society has for many years also presented Spring "music hall".

Abertillery Orpheus Ladies Choir, at Llangollen International Eisteddfod, 1950. The conductor was Mrs Moore and the accompanist, Mrs Watkins.

The Abertillery Orpheus Ladies Choir at St John's Church, Six Bells, c.1970. The choir was first formed in 1911 under the conductorship of Mr Tom Bundred (see p.148). During the Second World War it was reformed; several concerts were held at the Drill Hall in Abertillery and the money raised was used to provide comforts for the troops. Over the years the choirs has had many long serving members, including Anne Hale, who was accompanist for almost thirty years. At present the choir has about 45 members and practices at the Ebenezer Chapel. All concerts given are for charity.

Performance of *The Magic Key*, Somerset Street Church schoolroom, 1950s.

Abertillery Sea Cadets band, Six Bells, c.1958. From left to right: Terry Maggs, John Hooper, Lawrence Fieldhouse, Martin Pagett, David Maggs, -?-, J. Aylesbury, Martin Jones, Bandmaster Mervyn Wilkins from Blaina, Don Bearcroft, -?-, Michael Kelly.

Arael Griffin Gleemen formed c.1950 seen here in 1957. From left to right, back row: R. Lane, F. Jones, W. Thompson, E. Pratley, G. Griffiths, K. Edwards. Third row: B. Frost, K. Frampton, F. Mitchel, A. Trigg, D. Davies, A. James, M. Williams, S. Thompson. Second row: C. Blacker, N. Liddington, M. Frampton, C. Brimble, B. Trigg, B. Purnell, J. Upcott, D. Lane. Bottom row: A. Poore, U. Verrier (President), M. Brewer, W. Jones (Chairman of Abertillery U.D.C.), E. Richards (Secretary), J. Bryant (pianist), A. Cook (conductor).

Abertillery Boys Choir, winner of first prize at the 1959 Mid-Somerset Festival.

Abertillery Youth Choir surround their conductor, Mr Arthur Cook, a very influential figure in the choral history of the area, 1965.

Abertillery Orpheus Male Choir, Tabernacle Chapel, c.1968. The choir was founded in 1908 by members of the Trinity Church, Abertillery and the first meeting was held at Jackson's ice cream parlour, a favourite rendezvous in those days. The first conductor was Mr Tom Bundred and he was to shape the successful early development of the choir until his death in 1937. He was followed by Mr Ivor Screen (conductor between 1937 and 1942), Mrs Laura Edmunds-Jones(1942–1956), Mr Arthur Cook and Mr W.J. Easy (1956–60), Mrs Olga Guley (1960–69) and Mr Martin Budd (1969-present). The early choir consisted mainly of members of the area's church choirs, which flourished at the time, the majority of the choristers being employed in local coal mines. Concerts were given at local schools and churches and money was raised for many different charities, a task which is still carried out to great effect by the present choir. Over the years the Orpheus has performed in several important venues all over the world, most notably in St Peter's Square, Rome in 1982 where they sang for Pope John Paul II and thousands of Easter pilgrims. In 1992–93 the choir took part in the Ten Thousand Voices concerts at the National Stadium in Cardiff. Television and radio broadcasts have also been frequent and since 1983 three recordings have been produced: *The Tillery Sound* (1983), *With a Voice of Singing* (1987) and *By Request* (1991).

Ten
Sporting Life

Powell's Tillery gymnastic team, winners of the Welsh Amateur Gynastic Shield, 1905–6. From left to right, back row: G. Turner, J. Matthews, J. Probert. Second row: G. Hoskins (pianist), J. Mayled, W. Conley, H. Gill (Captain), W. Moore, W.F. Talbot, W. Jones (Honorary Secretary). Front row: T. Hill, C.W. Spalding (Instructor), W. Cowhig (Vice-Captain), E.L. Watkins. Cross-legged: G. Mead, G. Howells.

Abertillery Harriers, c.1908. From left to right, back row: A. Jukes (Head Trainer), J. Doyle Sr., A. Chaplin (Secretary), J. Pope, W. Silverthorne, E. Stead, F.J.H. Berrow (Treasurer), W. Matthews, G. Gapper, T. Wilshire, H. Read, W. Edmunds (Assistant Trainer). Front row: W.J.

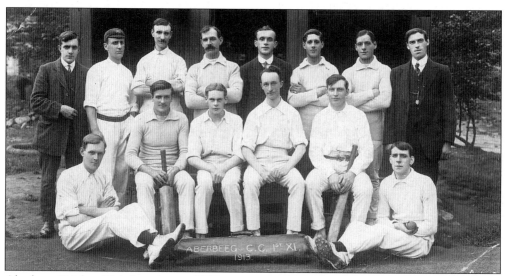

Aberbeeg Cricket Club first eleven, 1913.

Codd (Chairman), W.R. Parsons (Vice-Captain), J. Pavey (Captain), Dr Instance, E.J. Williams, Esq., J.P. (President and Chairman of Abertillery Urban District Council, 1903–04), J. Doyle (Vice-Captain), P. Mason, T. Newton. Cross-legged: S. Clarke, A. Jukes.

Quoits at Llanhilleth Park, 1934. The Park was opened here in 1924 when the course of the river was altered allowing for the development of football and cricket pitches, a bowls green and a quoits bed.

Six Bells bowls team, c.1930. From left to right, front row: David Thomas, Harry Hoskins, Alf Reed, Cliff Price, W.J. Harrington (Captain), Lewis Morgan, ? Boulton, ? Downs, "Talgarth" Williams.

Powell's Tillery Institute draughts club, Monmouthshire and District League champions, 1933–4 season. From left to right, back row: J. Morse, E. Wiggle, T. Thomas, F. Parfitt, J. Lloyd. Middle row: C. Pritchard (Vice-Chairman), A. Arnold, C. Lloyd, B. Edwards, R. Cox, G. Baker (Vice-Captain), Leon Reason (Secretary). Front row: G. Brookes, T. Waites, T. Coles (Captain) H. Stuart, T. Herbert. Left inset: Superintendent R. Baker D.C.C. Right inset: W.H. Gilson.

Abertillery County School rugby team, 1934–35 season.

"Pushball" team at the Aberbeeg Hospital garden fete, June 1936. From left to right, back row: A. Summerhill, E. Boots, B. James, G. Gay, B. Brown, C. Leigh. Middle row: E. Wathen, W. Evans, W. Davies, B. Snellgrove. Front row: W. Morris (kneeling left), G. Evans, C. Llewellyn (kneeling right).

Victorious water polo team from Powell's Tillery Swimming Club, 1948. From left to right, back row: Don Williams, G. Samuels, Ted Horler (Trainer), Reg Hanney, Gordon Lewis. Seated: Les Selwyn, Reg Jones, Reg Hoskins (Captain), Cyril Crook, Ellis Rowlands (Secretary). Cross-legged: Cliff Roberts, Ted Jeffries. Reg Hoskins, a powerful swimmer who often took part in river races, was called on by the police to assist in the search when somebody was reported drowned locally, for example in Pen-y-fan Pond. This he did without the benefit of the breathing apparatus which today's "cossetted" frogmen have to aid the recovery of bodies. In 1924, Reg's father, 47 year old haulier Richard Hoskins was killed at the same Gray pit in Abertillery in which his son was working. A broken rope had caused a runaway journey (train) of colliery trams but instead of looking after his own safety Mr Hoskins made a courageous attempt to warn his butties, who were working further down the track, of the oncoming danger. In so doing he was run over and killed. This act of heroism was subsequently recognized by the Carnegie Hero Fund Trust which paid his widow a gratuity of one pound a week during her lifetime.

In 1948 a second local man, Arthur Bobbett of Woodland Terrace, Aberbeeg also earned a Carnegie Award for his bravery underground at the Six Bells Colliery. On 21 October 1948 Arthur, an ambulanceman at the pit, risked his life trying to free a young miner who had been trapped by a roof fall at the coal face. He laboured for three-quarters of an hour in hazardous conditions working to saw through the timber collars which were pinning the man down. Sadly, despite this extraordinary effort the man once freed was found to be already dead. Bobbett, however, never lived to receive his Carnegie certificate, nor the Edward Medal or the Daily Herald Order of Industrial Heroism which his actions had merited. On 19 November that same year he, too, was killed by a roof fall at Six Bells. His medals, awarded posthumously, are now in the care of Abertillery Museum, having been presented to the society by the Bobbett family.

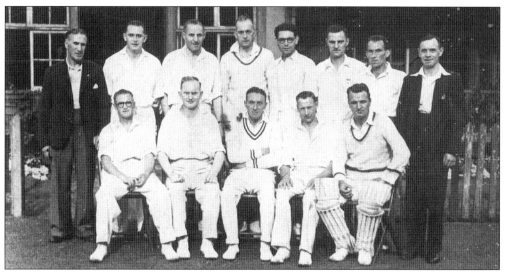

Llanhilleth Cricket Club, 1949. From left to right, back row: O.J. Rogers (Secretary for 30 years), Roy Morgan, Bryn Jeremiah, Tom Edwards, Arthur Sargeant, Walter Rogers, Arthur Davies, Bill Lewis (umpire). Front row: Arthur Hill, Cliff Maxwell, Fred Beames, Bert Challenger, Oliver Rogers. The club's original home was "Jobbie Jaynes Field" but in the early 1920s it moved to its present ground in Llanhilleth Park. In 1965 Llanhilleth shared the Monmouthshire Cricket Association League Championship with Newport A.C. and were runners-up in the Challenge Shield cup final in 1962 and 1964. The present Secretary (since 1955) is Phillip Maggs.

Monmouthshire Police Sports, Abertillery Park, 1948. A wet track caused havoc for other competitors; on the ground nearest the grass is Reg Baynham of Abertillery, winner of the previous years's event and Johnny Dennis of Norwood Paragon R.C., a talented rider who broke his collar bone in the fall thereby losing his chance of a place in the British team for the 1948 Olympic Games held in London. Three years earlier, in 1945, however, a far more tragic accident had occured when Cwmcarn rider, Jim Wood was killed after crashing and hitting his head on a pedal. Held annually each summer at Abertillery Park, the Monmouthshire Police Sports was a major meeting for cyclists and athletes and drew large crowds. Races were interspersed by various novelty events and displays by trick motor cyclists. In recent years the cycle track, which was laid in 1906, has been allowed to deteriorate and although still in place it can no longer be used for racing.

Annual dinner of Abertillery and District Wheelers cycling club held at the Bush Hotel, 15 January 1955. The club, formed in 1945, is still a very active organisation known throughout Wales. As the only remaining cycling club in the Borough of Blaenau Gwent it draws members from a wide catchment area.

Abertillery R.F.C, 1950–51 season. From left to right, back row: M. Davies, G. Bridge, O. Jenkins, R. Paul, I. Williams, G. Davies, R. Norster, M. Evans. Middle row: E. Coleman, N. Bevan, K. Morley, B. Jones (Captain), W. Griffin, R. Rees, T. Bowen. Front row: R. Williams, J. Hollyfield, T. Rees, R. Cecil.

View of The Park, home of Abertillery R.F.C., 1961. To the north beyond the park, in the shadow of its waste, is Rose Heyworth Colliery. Note also the old grandstand to the rugby pitch (the new stand was built in 1965).

Aberbeeg R.F.C., 1961–62 season. The captain that year was Ron Lloyd and the mascot, his son, Dafydd. Also pictured are John Reece, Brian Lane, Jack Clarke, Bob Fowler, Ron Turner, Brian Woodland and John Thayer.

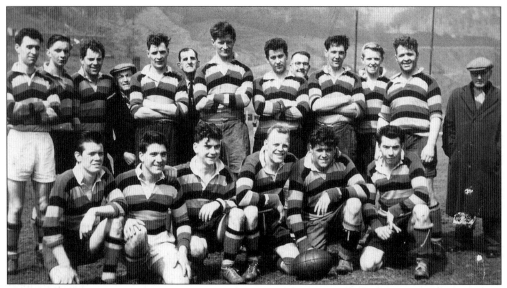

Blaenau Gwent R.F.C., 1962–63. From left to right, back row: Colin Francis, Dai Williams, Alan Jones, Albert York, Bernard Evans, Danny Lee, Ray Davies, Gary Stevens, Charlie Mason, Billy Thomas, Terry Taylor, Harvey Pugh, Dai Watkins (senior committeeman). Front row: Glyn Williams, Colin Rees, Cyril Lewis, Norman Liddington, Cliff Blanchard, Ervin Williams. The club was officially founded in 1869 and lays claim to the honour of being the oldest rugby club in Wales. Since 1927, the club's permanent ground has been at Abertillery Park.

Llanhilleth R.F.C., 1967–68. This season (1994–5) the club is celebrating its centenary with Michael Attwell, the mascot pictured above, the captain for the year! From left to right, back row: A Parker, R. Rogers, T. Minchin, N. Sansom, E. Newman, M. Sweet, C. Burgwin, P. Woodland, D. Rogers, T. Williams, I Davies (Treasurer). Second row: G. Attwell, M. Williams, H. Hewins (Chairman), B. Collier (Captain), J. Thomas (Secretary), N. Thomas, M. Yates. Front row: R. Lewis, M. Attwell (mascot), B. Hayes. In 1961 Norman Morgan became the first Llanhilleth player to be capped at senior international level for Wales, playing on three occasions against Scotland, Ireland and France.

The former Walpole Hotel, Llanhilleth, headquarters of the rugby club since 1978.

Cwmtillery R.F.C. 2nd XV, winners of the Harvey Morris Memorial Cup, 1991–92.

Acknowledgements

I would like to thank everyone who has loaned pictures or given us information and advice during the preparation of this book. It has been a pleasure to work with you all. If I had been able to include all the material which was loaned then I don't think anyone would have been able to lift the book!

My special thanks go to Don and Peggy Bearcroft for their support and hospitality, Mr Bert Snellgrove for providing an excellent foreword and to Mrs Pam Hopkins, a most valuable source of ideas.

Betty Arndell, Chris Arnold, Cllr Graham Bartlett (Clerk of Abertillery Community Council), Reg Baynham, Lyn Bearcroft, Barbara Bevan, Mrs Carol Brooks and the staff of Abertillery Primary School, Bob Challenger and Llanhilleth R.F.C., Joyce Coombes, Ruth Curtis, Mr Emmanuel (Ash's), Jesse Evans, Bob Fowler, Brian Fry, Lyn Gladwyn, Mrs Holland and the staff and residents of Cwrt Mytton, J. Homer, Gwyneth Howells, John Hughes, Gary Hulme, Bernard Jones, Bernard Jones (Abertillery R.F.C.), John Jones, Joyce Jones, Morfydd Jones, Arthur Lewis O.B.E., Jean Lewis, Phillip Maggs and Llanhilleth Cricket Club, Anne Maund and the staff of the Abertillery Library, Mr & Mrs Morgan, Frank Olding, Bob Pitt, Chris Poore and Blaenau Gwent R.F.C., Don Powell, George Price, Haydn Rees, John Rees, H. Reynolds, Hazel Robinson, Ralph Robinson, Janice and Roy Rogers, Gordon Rowlands, John Selway, Dorothy Snellgrove, Mike and Arline Stowermark, Andrew J. Tidey, David Warren, Lyndon Watkins, Jim Watkins, Mrs E. Wiles, Shirley Winmill (Historian of Abertillery Operatic Society).

Please allow me to apologize in advance to anyone who helped and yet has not been included in the above list. Any omissions or errors in the text, meanwhile, are my responsiblity alone.

Abertillery and District Museum Society has a long and successful tradition of safeguarding the heritage of the area. I hope that anyone who is looking for a secure home for their photographs, postcards and other memorabilia from the area's past, will think of the Museum and allow them to continue this labour of love.

The Dog stone on the mountain between Cwmtillery and Blaenavon, 1992. This was erected by Thomas Kennard, builder of Crumlin Viaduct, in memory of his dog, which he had accidently shot on the first day of the grouse shooting season in 1864.